How Do
I Know?

Your Guide to Decision-Making Mastery

Annita Keane

BALBOA.
PRESS
A DIVISION OF HAY HOUSE

Balboa Press books may be ordered through booksellers or by contacting:

Balboa Press
A Division of Hay House
1663 Liberty Drive
Bloomington, IN 47403
www.balboapress.com
1 (877) 407-4847

Because of the dynamic nature of the Internet, any web addresses or links contained in this book may have changed since publication and may no longer be valid. The views expressed in this work are solely those of the author and do not necessarily reflect the views of the publisher, and the publisher hereby disclaims any responsibility for them.

The author of this book does not dispense medical advice or prescribe the use of any technique as a form of treatment for physical, emotional, or medical problems without the advice of a physician, either directly or indirectly. The intent of the author is only to offer information of a general nature to help you in your quest for emotional and spiritual well-being. In the event you use any of the information in this book for yourself, which is your constitutional right, the author and the publisher assume no responsibility for your actions.

Any people depicted in stock imagery provided by Thinkstock are models, and such images are being used for illustrative purposes only. Certain stock imagery © Thinkstock.

Printed in the United States of America.

ISBN: 978-1-4525-2352-1 (sc)
ISBN: 978-1-4525-2354-5 (hc)
ISBN: 978-1-4525-2353-8 (e)

Library of Congress Control Number: 2014918125

Balboa Press rev. date: 11/19/2014

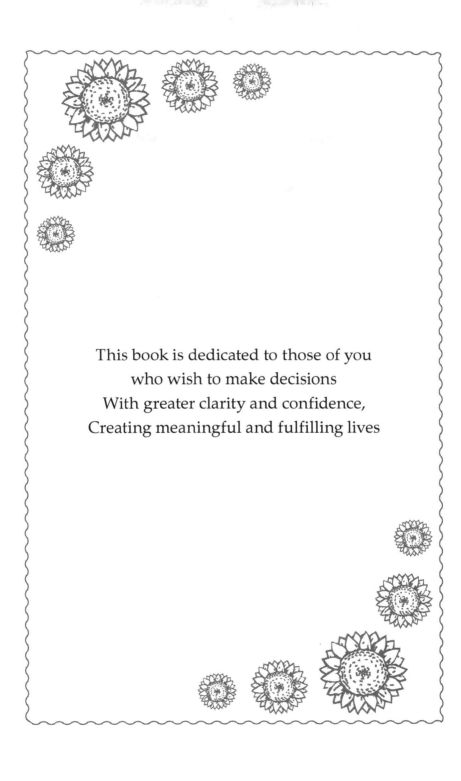

This book is dedicated to those of you
who wish to make decisions
With greater clarity and confidence,
Creating meaningful and fulfilling lives

Acknowledgements

I wish to thank my partner and best friend Larry,
Son Larry and Daughter Emma
For their continued patience and
support throughout this project.

Contents

Introduction

Do you have difficulty deciding what you want? Do you get confused trying to find relationships that work for you? Have you ever wondered why you struggle to decide the steps needed for change? Have you ever been unhappy with the results when you made a decision based on what others recommended? Have you pursued someone else's dream, thinking it was yours? Have you had a hunch and overridden it with logic, only to find you missed a big opportunity? Have you asked your friends and "experts" for guidance, researched as much as you could, and just ended up more confused than ever?

And have you ever acted on a hunch, knowing you were right (without a logical explanation), and created great success?

If any of the above is true for you, you are reading the right book.

The most frequent question I've been asked in my eight years as an intuitive healer and coach is "How do I know I'm making the right decision?"

Even though we are living in the Information Age, when books and almost universal access to the Internet provide access to consultants with valuable advice on every topic imaginable, we still struggle to make decisions in the crucial areas of life. We find ourselves repeatedly asking "How do I know" questions like these:

- How do I know which advice is best for me?
- How do I know he/she is "the one"?
- How do I know if I love him/her?
- How do I know if it's time to leave him/her?
- How do I know if it's time to change careers?
- How do I make a decision for someone else, like a child or an elderly parent?
- How do I know if my fear is reasonable or unreasonable?
- How do I know that I can trust myself?

We know that many factors influence our decisions in answering these "How do I know" questions for good or bad. But did you know that we get what we *believe* in our lives, and not necessarily what we *want*. If your reality doesn't match your dreams—that is, if your experiences are not what you want—it is likely that you have made decisions based on old programming, and that has led you to your current reality.

"Old programming" is a term I use to explain the stories, beliefs, and ideas that we learn growing up. For example, you might find yourself saying things your mother said, or you respond the same way as your father in certain circumstances. While you may not buy these old beliefs intellectually, they can be submerged in your subconscious and show up in the results of your life.

The good news is that there are many ways to uncover what stops you from making the decisions that will lead you toward realizing your dreams. One way is to spend time uncovering your old programs, which are those of your parents and peers that you have bought into. But how do you uncover them since most are buried in your subconscious? After all, *subconscious* means that you are unaware of the thinking. So why are such thoughts so elusive?

The subconscious mind stores every experience as well as every thought, feeling, and sense you have about that experience. When you learn a new skill, like riding a bike, at first there are many things to remember. As cycling becomes more familiar to you, you start to cycle automatically. Why is this? Your subconscious mind stores all the details you no longer need to call to your conscious mind. You don't have to think about how to cycle anymore; you *know* how to cycle. This happens with every skill you learn; you don't need to remember all the details. So a subconscious thought is one that has become so familiar, you don't know you are thinking it. The same goes for what you have learned from your parents, caregivers, and others.

So you don't have to remember everything, because your subconscious mind runs 24/7, influencing your decisions without you noticing—until you are unhappy with your results, that is. I will be teaching you skills to access your subconscious programs later in chapter 9.

Another way of making better decisions is taking back your power and coming from your authentic self. Up until now, you may have learned to look outside yourself for answers—to your parents or teachers, religious or spiritual leaders, doctors or politicians, and even the Internet. These make great recommendations, and doing what they say can work well. However, they tend to recommend what works well for *them*. That may not necessarily apply to what you want to do or what you want to achieve.

The trouble starts when you pay more attention to what others say than to your own voice. As you grew up, you learned to behave a certain way and might have gotten into trouble for being yourself. You learned to move from trusting your body sense to trusting your head, as you figured out who you should be rather than who you are in order to fit in. You got positive acknowledgement for that. Before long, you started to act in a way that made others happy, and you became afraid to be yourself and afraid of what others thought of you. In chapter 10 we explore taking action from your authentic self.

A third way of making better-informed decisions is to tap into your inner wisdom. Most people constantly live in emergency mode. We call it stress: avoiding and/or fighting against something or someone to survive. The head is designed to make decisions in emergency situations. The gut, heart, and body senses are designed to contain your inner wisdom. Working as your natural navigation system, combining your head and your physical senses allow you to be more able to make the decisions that will work for you. They guide you to your life path, and the degree of connection determines your personal *power*, in the true sense of the word.

You may have heard this referred to as emotional intelligence, intuition, or gut instinct. It shows up in your life in the simplest ways. Your emotions or feelings are your responses to a thought. It is easy to misinterpret these feelings, as most of us haven't learned how to interpret them yet. The more ease you feel, the easier it is to connect with your inner wisdom. The more conflicted you are, the more difficult it is. In other words, when stressed you are disconnected from your gut instincts.

Is it any wonder you have difficulty with decisions? You have learned to disconnect your inner knowing (body wisdom) from your outer learning. And you engage in a way that is oriented toward surviving whatever comes at you in the day. By learning how to connect your mind and your senses, you can begin to be intentional during your day, to manage it, to create it as the power that you are. You become clearer on what works for you, and your decisions become a whole lot easier.

- **You have a unique set of answers within that only you can discern for yourself.**
- **No one can tell you what works best for you better than you can.**
- **Each decision you make maps out the direction of your life.**
- **'Give a man a fish and you feed him for a day; teach a man to fish and you feed him for life'**

The statements in the box above reflect my own philosophy on life and coaching. I was originally trained as a scientist, and I worked in hospitals in Ireland and England. My world was well defined by what I had learned. I knew who I was and where I was going. As far as making decisions were concerned, I did what I knew to do—what I had learned to do. But when I was unable to predict the outcome, I struggled without an external reference point to guide me, unaware that I could deliberately connect within. I often knew what I could do or should do, but I was unable to establish if it would work for me. Only when I changed my career to coaching and developed my skills in energy work, psychotherapy, and the like did I become aware that I could deliberately connect with this inner knowing.

There were more aspects to decision making than I had thought. As I worked with my clients, I found that there are five things to consider when making decision: thoughts, emotions, the physical senses, the subconscious, and the spiritual. And, very simply, there are two types of decisions: those where you are connected to your inner wisdom (gut instinct) and those where you are not. When I made my decisions in a disconnected place, I almost always second-guessed myself. I often missed the moment because I would worry, *Did I make the right decision?* or *What if things go wrong?* Does this sound familiar? This even applies to simple things like what we eat or drink. When you connect to your gut instinct when eating, it will let you know if this food works for you. An obvious example is when the food doesn't suit you, you may experience bloating, indigestion, or heartburn.

In this book, I will teach you how to tune in to your whole intelligence—intellectual, emotional, physical, and spiritual—so that you can intuit your answers from the inside out. You will learn how to read your life circumstance and how to make sense of it. Everything you encounter will become a tool for living and learning, rather than confusing details that keep you stuck in merely existing and coping with everyday living.

You can start to make decisions that work for you by learning

- how to connect with your instincts;
- how to utilize all the information available to you;
- how to use your apparent mistakes and transform them into assets; and
- how to identify and rule out details, emotions, and beliefs that may be distracting you from making the decisions that really matter.

My wish is that this book will help you make decisions that allow you to play the lead role in your story.

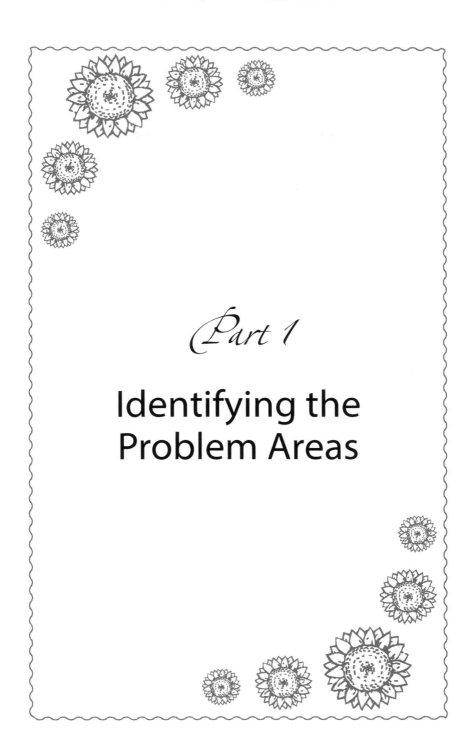

Part 1

Identifying the
Problem Areas

Chapter One

The Importance of Decision Making

> To *decide* is to eliminate options in order to focus actions on the direction of your choice. Paraphrased from the *Oxford English Dictionary*

*W*hat is showing up in your life today is a direct result of the decisions you have made up to now. In order to create a different result you have to make a different decision.

There are times when it makes sense to follow what others are doing or to get advice; there are also times when only you know what is best for you, regardless of what makes logical sense or what others say. It's these decisions I struggled with the most. As a result, I felt stuck—a lot! I would avoid making a decision. Sometimes I was afraid I would do the wrong thing.

Sometimes I was afraid of losing a friend or a partner or a job. Most of the time, I was afraid to make a decision and afraid *not* to make one at the same time. This kept me in a state of doing nothing.

Often, the only way I would make a decision was if life nudged me to do so. In other words, my back was against the wall before I decided. This made life more difficult than it needed to be. Finally, I grew tired of getting not-so-friendly nudges from the universe and decided that my life could be a little easier.

While I became aware of gut instinct, I didn't know how to connect with it on purpose. You know when you *know* what to do next. It just feels right. You feel sure, and there is no doubt whatsoever. That is when your thoughts, emotions, and gut instincts are all on the same page, or aligned. I was aware that when I was in this sure place, the outcomes of my decisions worked well for my family and me.

But at times I would get significant opposition from friends and family. "What are you doing? Are you crazy?" they'd say. Though my decisions looked like I was passing up an opportunity, they always, always paid off, setting me up in a better position than I had been in previously. I am glad I persisted. This happened in career moves, with partner decisions, and when buying property. In these situations, if and when things worked out, I believed I was lucky.

Very simply, I learned from examples like those given above that there are two types of decisions: those where you are connected to your inner wisdom and those where you are not. When I made my decisions from that disconnected place, I almost always second-guessed myself. I often missed the opportunity because I would worry, procrastinate, and wonder if things would go wrong. I was hoping for the best and doubting myself at the same time. Does this sound familiar?

The inability to make decisions makes you a product of your environment rather than master of your world. When you don't know what you want, others decide for you. This is fine for a kid, but it doesn't work when you want to take control of your life.

Choosing your life goals and making decisions that direct your actions to achieve those goals keeps you from becoming the victim of your life. Discovering the ability to decide and take the steps to achieve what you want is *critical* to you taking charge of your direction in the world.

When you were a child, you were told what to do, and you lived according to others' rules. As you moved into your teenage years, you started to make decisions for yourself. You had the guidance of your parents, teachers, and peers, and you learned how to develop your choices and then decided according to the directions you chose. As you progressed, your decisions were based on knowing what you wanted. Now, even in work, you need to have plans or goals that align with the company but are yours nonetheless.

Decisions determine the actions you take to create the outcomes you want. Where you live and with whom, where you go, what you do, and where you work are all results of decisions. Your decisions determine whether or not you take the steps necessary to achieve your goals. They cause you to stay the same or to change direction. Have you noticed that the main reason you get stuck in something is because of the difficulty of deciding what to do next?

You can have many great ideas, but if you don't make decisions to take action, the great ideas remain just that—ideas. For example, have you had a great idea and not taken action, only to see someone else make a lot of money out of it later on?

Knowing What You Want

Knowing what you want is important when making decisions. The more clearly you can specify what you want, the better the chance you have of making decisions that lead straight there. Say, for example, you want to meet a new partner. The decision supporting that want sets the actions necessary to make that happen. You may decide to join a dating agency. You probably have a good idea of what you would like your partner to be like. And as you begin the dating process, the experiences help you to further discern your ideal partner. You also develop a definite set of no's and an extensive list of yes's.

Knowing What You Don't Want

Sometimes it is easier to know what you do want based on knowing what you don't want. Knowing what you don't want helps you to fine-tune what you do want. You can make decisions that define the steps you need to take in the direction you want or to take away from what you don't want. For example, you may start your education with a general science degree. As you learn more about the subject, you can better choose the direction you would prefer to specialize in, like biochemistry or physics. When you are stuck, making the decision to move in any direction can shift your status quo.

Thinking You Know What You Want

While you can make decisions based on others' experiences and advice, it may not give you the satisfaction you thought it would. If you are a teenager, when you develop more independence, there are so many things to learn and so many first times, it can be scary. It is easy to go for what you know and to follow your parents or peers. Some decide to rebel against their parents and peers. The reality is that only you can determine your likes and dislikes. And working out the pieces you want to keep and those you want to leave behind is a natural part of growing up.

So set a goal. The decisions you make will determine your path to that goal. The power of decision making comes in having the ability to change your mind if something isn't working and to set a course in a different direction. It is knowing when to change course or not, depending on the circumstances. While the logistics of changing those decisions isn't always easy, the fear of making mistakes or repeating old mistakes can be a real concern. It's okay to change your mind and your direction. Often, continuing what you are doing when you know it's *not* working can do more harm than good.

Decisions—especially the big ones, such as regarding a partner or career—shape your life. And you have to make them without knowing the outcome. So many factors are out of your control. But one thing we can all do as human beings is make the best decision we can under the circumstances. Old hurts and unhappy experiences can leave you fearful and hesitant about making decisions. Maybe you landed in the job from hell or in an unhappy partnership, or you botched your finances. The fears caused by these can affect how you make new decisions. You might run from the pain and become less and less inclined to change or to decide to enter into a new opportunity. Why? You are afraid that the next decision will create the same result as the last one and that you will get hurt again.

There is always some reason for you to decide in the first place—for example, a change in circumstances, wanting to improve your lifestyle, a new job, a potential partner, a health problem, or even something as simple as an unexpected change of plans. Life changes all the time, so you need to adjust your course regularly. Your decisions determine every outcome in your world, and you get to make them on a daily basis.

The question is, what do you use as a compass? You're outer or your inner world—or both? Which do you rely on the most?

"Your ability to connect all the information available to your gut instinct and inner wisdom is the secret to making decisions that consistently work in your favor."

Getting this right can open you into creating the life of your dreams. Think of the time, energy, and money you can save by moving in a direction of ease and flow within, instead of going on a wild goose chase, trying to live according to someone else's rules.

But first you must understand why decisions can be such a struggle.

Chapter Two

Why We Struggle with Decisions

> If my attachment to what I know blinds
> me to all the available options, then my
> knowledge is controlling me; it is controlling
> my intention, and it is creating my personal
> Dream for me. But with awareness of my
> attachments comes the opportunity to take
> back that control and to live as I choose.
> Don Miguel Ruiz Jr., *The Five
> Levels of Attachment*

We all learn to override our instincts and natural wisdom to fit in with the tribe. So you have learned to look outside yourself for answers. Do you struggle to believe in yourself as a result? You may not have learned how to trust yourself in the first place. Do you believe that what others say is more important than what you have to say? Based on past experience, you may also struggle to believe others.

Making decisions is a complex process. So many factors have to be considered. You would think that with so much information available, you would have no problem making decisions. If anything, information makes things more confusing. There are so many options, how do you decide what will work for you?

Having learned to look to others for answers, you may not know how to go within as a reference point. When we were kids, we accepted a lot of what we were told. There is nothing wrong with this; we have to start somewhere. But as we grow into adulthood, there always seems to be someone who knows the answer, or who knows better. Have you noticed how many gurus and experts are out there? There is only one problem with that: the only person who knows what you want is *you*. And if you don't know how to connect with your inner wisdom to be clear on that, what do you do?

There is a good chance you are out there chasing your parents', your cultures, or others' ideas of what your dreams should be or could be. Let's face it, we all are—or were at some point. And you may not even be aware of it. Is it any wonder fulfillment is out of your reach?

Our instincts often conflict with what we have learned—and this is *supposed* to happen. Your peers and elders provided you with the framework that worked for them, and it is up to you to incorporate it into your life in a way that works for you. This inner conflict motivates you to question what you learned and to open up to the possibilities that can work for you. Most of us misinterpret what this conflict means, getting caught up in the drama. Basically, we learn to override our instincts to fit in with our tribe. And the conflict may actually be telling you that this worked for your parent but doesn't work for you.

It is easy to lose trust when we get advice that doesn't help. We learn that others know better (or should know better). We lose trust when others deliberately lead us astray for their gain and at our expense. And we lose trust when we believed an influential someone and it turns out he or she was lying all along. You also learn to lose trust in yourself when you are trying to be one thing for your parents, another for your teacher, and someone else again for your friends and colleagues. Where does it end?

You will need to relearn how to trust yourself.

You may know this already. Or you may think, *Oh, is that what that is?* Learning how to trust yourself greatly enhances your decision-making process. That trust makes it easier to commit to taking the steps required to move in the direction of a decision, because you relearn how to read your own signals.

Traditionally, we have learned to make our decisions based on the information available at the time. We picked up ideas from our parents and others. But truth is relative to the perceiver, and this makes looking outside for your answers very confusing. Really, you could ask ten different experts and get ten different opinions; therefore, it is important you make your decisions based on what is true for you.

Because we have such easy access to information; old, rigid belief systems are starting to crumble. What you believe to be true today may no longer be relevant for you tomorrow. That's evolution. Your decisions change accordingly.

When you were very young, you lived by your family's rules. When you left home, you developed your own rules. Were they different? Some you adopted from home and some you created yourself. How does this affect your decisions? It is *your* life. You are living it. How can someone else make your decisions? The rules that affected you as a child are no longer relevant today, and yet many of your decisions today are based on your childhood experiences. How many of the rules you learned as a child are still running your life now? The results show up in your life.

Decision-making can be difficult because of our attachment to the familiar. The second reason is that we just don't like change because of emotional attachments. The combination keeps us stuck like hamsters on wheels.

When we don't like aspects of our lives and are afraid to—or believe we can't—change them; our decisions and actions then may become the result of a fear or belief rather than being fully informed by all the information available. The result? More of the same. We are attached to what is familiar.

Have you noticed that the number-one thing human beings hate is change? I have spoken to many clients over the years, and the most common theme I encounter is that they want to change their lives yet they don't want to change what they are doing. But if you continue to do the same things in the same way, how can you achieve a different result?

Would you believe that your body is in constant motion? Your energy dynamics are always changing. Your emotions are constantly changing. The only thing that is not changing is your thought process.

And you become used to thinking in a certain way. The old ways are difficult to change because you become attached to the way you think and to how you do things. The feeling of familiarity enfolds you like a security blanket, regardless of whether that familiarity actually works for you or not.

Our thoughts generate a chain reaction in our body, which culminates in our body taking action—or not. So when we think a certain thought, we engage the loop of physiological, emotional, energetic, and physical responses that leads to the behavior that creates our external experience. When we need to do things a certain way, this becomes a loop of habit. Like a hamster on a hamster wheel, once you jump on, you continue doing and reacting to the same events or people in the same way. This is great if it works for you. If not, making a different decision is what will make a difference in the result.

You can develop an unhealthy comfort zone in your body by ignoring or misreading signals that say you are out of your comfort zone. Say, for example, you notice a twinge in your lower back. You rub it and take a painkiller, and the pain goes away for a while. You curb your activities slightly and forget about it as soon as the pain dissipates. Before long, you are back at normal activities.

A few weeks later, after a round of golf, you feel the twinge again. It is a little more noticeable this time. Again you take painkillers and forget about it when the pain disappears. It takes a little longer to get back to normal, and you notice you are compromising your posture a little to protect your back. You soon forget about that.

A month later you are in the garden, pulling a stubborn weed. Just as it releases from the ground, you notice something pop in your lower back. You can't straighten up. An hour later, you find yourself at a chiropractor's or doctor's office, and you say, "It just popped, out of the blue. I never saw it coming."

As time passed, you went from a twinge to a slipped disc, because you create different comfort zones to accommodate the pain. The changes were so small that the gradual shift from "just a twinge" to a slipped disc was almost imperceptible.

Finding comfort in our discomfort zone is how we develop illnesses. It is also how life crises creep up on us as we ignore our personal alarm system called *stress*. The cumulative effects of stress can go unnoticed for a long time. And the more we discover, the more we realize stress is the underlying culprit for so much disease. Stress is an indicator that you are out of balance.

You may find the same thing happening in your relationships. You do things the way you always do, ignoring the warning signals. Before you know it, you've grown apart and wonder how that happened. Maybe you were busy or distracted with work or with your kids' activities, taking the other for granted. It feels like it crept up on you. You are not sure what you should do differently. We learned how to be in relationships from a very young age, and sometimes we relate through how we think we should be rather than who we are. You can see how easy it is to disconnect.

My point is that learned behavior doesn't necessarily serve us. Your body is signaling these imbalances all the time, just as it does when you're hungry or tired. You may not have learned how to read these signals yet. The signals that are saying, "Pay attention." The signals that tell you that you are moving out of balance.

If you are like most people, your reply might be, "I will deal with that later" or "Where are the painkillers?" And it feels like the illness, relationship crisis, or work incident just happened out of the blue. As you learn to connect the dots between the thought, the emotion, and the physical sense, you will be able to make a decision to take remedial action much earlier than in the past. You might alleviate the crisis or leave the offending situation much sooner than you would have in the past.

Life is a dynamic process. Persistently doing things that don't work for you, rather than growing and developing with the natural changes of life, has a way of catching up with you. When you learn to listen, you will realize that your body had been warning you for quite some time. If you learned to do things that don't work from day one, you won't even know they don't work for you. By trying to stay the same and by ignoring the signals, you learned to accommodate the malfunction. And rather than renegotiate to adjust to the changes, you renegotiate to keep things the same—at your expense. You don't have to be an addict to be caught in a pattern. You just have to be attached to doing things or feeling things in a certain way.

Here's the thing: we can confuse genuine balance and harmony with our comfort zone. We can be in an unhealthy situation and, knowing no different, *feel* balanced and in harmony, or at least content. This is not the same as balance and harmony. The Eastern gurus talk about a life of nonattachment and the calm that ensues. In my experience, our understanding of balance is related more to our comfort zone than to true balance. For example, most people with heartburn take an antacid. But heartburn means that the food or drink they consumed doesn't agree with their digestive system. Instead of reducing the quantity of or cutting out the offending food, they increase the antacids and continue eating.

A more sobering example is growing up in an abusive household and continuing the legacy of abuse in your own family because you don't know any better. Or seeing your best friend go for the guy who is going to mess her up *again*. You see it clearly: she feels the familiarity of what "love" is to her. In other words, she has learned to associate love with a certain range of feelings and behaviors. How does this affect her decision? My guess is she falls headlong into the situation, regardless of what you say and regardless of her own alarm system. Until she learns to read those signals correctly, she will repeat the scenario again and again.

When your intellect, emotional intelligence, and physical intelligence are *not* aligned, decisions become a battle. You feel conflicted. Learning how to recognize your signals and learning to discern between balance and familiarity (again, the familiarity of what is not working) is key. Navigating the changes, decision by decision is much easier than we have been led to believe. It is exhausting to stay stuck in one drama after another. Wouldn't you prefer to use your energy to build the life of your dreams?

> You can't solve a problem at the
> level in which it was created.
> Albert Einstein

So our attachment to the familiar and our emotional attachments that keep us from changing need to be examined.

How Do I Know I Am Attached?

An attachment is anything that limits your options when you need to make decisions that impact your future or to change. We can be attached to people, things, and situations in a number of ways. Your beliefs can keep you attached to thinking a certain way. And your emotions can keep you attached to feeling a certain way or responding in an emotional way. Tradition and learned behaviors keep you attached to behaving a certain way. You may be afraid of losing someone, or you may believe you have to do things the way your parents did. You may love a house and location so much that you have trouble leaving, even when the logical thing to do is sell. I have a friend who preferred to remain unemployed rather than leave her beloved hometown.

You know some of your attachments; they are obvious. The problem is attachments you are not aware of. They are hidden under your conscious radar—in your subconscious. They are beliefs you aren't conscious of and fears that are many years old. Your adult mind isn't afraid; the fears are buried in your subconscious. You may find you attract the same type of partner over and over. You may be stuck in a dead-end job and wonder why you can't take the actions necessary to move on. You may have hit a plateau in a weight-loss program for no apparent reason. You may feel stuck in a rut, knowing there is something stopping you but not knowing what. In dieting, for example, you might try to force the change through willpower, not understanding the underlying attachments (beliefs, emotions, and so on) that are secretly opposing the change.

You can know your attachments only by looking at the results in your life, family, work, or friendships. The biggest clue to your secret attachments are incidents or relationships turning up in your life that you are unhappy with. Below are ways you can tell you are attached or hooked to something. Do any of these look familiar to you?

At the level of the mind:

➢ You can't think about anything else.
➢ You go over and over the story in your head.
➢ You find that you defend your point valiantly, needing to be right or to win.
➢ You find yourself judging the situation or relationship, making it wrong or right.
➢ You are confused.
➢ You have difficulty listening to another's point of view.
➢ You take another's point of view personally.

➤ You can think of only one way to approach the issue, and that is yours.

At the level of your emotions:

➤ You feel a strong emotional charge—anger, sadness, anxiety, desire—about the situation or person. (An event or relationship that is *charged* involves strong emotions, either positive or negative, connected with that event or relationship.)
➤ You fear losing your job, partner, house.
➤ You feel angry, frustrated, or anxious at certain times.

At the level of your body:

➤ You feel pain or tension in an area of your body.
➤ You notice a sense—not a pain—in different parts of your body, such as a constriction at your throat or a heaviness in your chest.
➤ You feel a sudden twinge or darting pain in an area of your body.
➤ You may notice your breathing has changed.
➤ You feel tense.
➤ You experience recurrent physical symptoms.

> You feel tired when you think or talk about the attachment.
> You find the situation draining; you feel sapped of energy.
> You feel highly energized at first and then exhausted (almost like a sugar rush).

At the level of the spirit:

> You remember this happening before, and you have no idea why it is still happening (repeating patterns).
> The outside world is telling you something.
> You are stuck in a conflict or a repeating pattern.
> The situation seems familiar.
> You keep meeting the same "type."

At the level of behavior:

> You find it difficult to let go.
> You consistently avoid a situation rather than deal with it.
> When things go wrong, your response is to eat, drink, or turn to some other habit.

➢ You are compelled to fix things, people, and situations, regardless of whether it is your place to do so.

➢ You react to situations rather than respond.

Now that you have an idea of how attachments present themselves, you need to determine what kind of decision maker you are. In the next chapter, you will see how your attachments affect your decision-making process.

Chapter Three

How Do You Make Decisions

What Is Problematic Decision Making?

Some decisions you make lead you to take the same steps in the same direction to results you don't want and problems you can do without. You may find yourself in a similar situation in every workplace, or you go out with the same type of man or woman, or you eat food that doesn't agree with you, or you leave a good relationship or stay in a bad relationship. You get my drift? Sometimes you know the decisions that you need to make to create that result; sometimes you don't.

How Do You Make Your Decisions?

The first step toward becoming a better decision maker is to establish what kind of decision maker you are right now. As you investigate your decision style, you may find you have developed it to protect a status quo, a way of thinking, or a way of doing things. It may be fueled by fear or by a belief that is no longer relevant to your life. You may simply do what you always do. See the ways of making decisions below, and establish which styles you use.

Do you take your time?

➢ Are you the deliberator? Do you engage in long and careful consideration? Do you mull over and over the facts and research everything you can find. Ask lots of friends and colleagues. Put a lot of work and time into making the right choice and subsequent decision.

➢ Do you ask everybody you know and chose the answer you like the most? Do you do this rather than considering what you actually want? Is your aim to make a popular decision?

➢ Do you ask everybody you know and argue with those who don't give you the answer you want?

➢ Have you already made up your mind and ask others because you think you should?

➢ Do you argue with others' answers because you need further convincing? Or do you use others' arguments to strengthen your reasons for making that decision in the first place.

Do you make reactive decisions?

➢ Do you make decisions based on your emotions, such as anger, fear, love, or joy. A typical example of this is in a work situation where you make a decision because you like or dislike a colleague rather than exercising professional judgment. Another example is "loving" someone so much that you can't see that he or she is not good for you, or you can see it and make the decision to be with that person anyway. In other words, do emotions cloud your ability to decide clearly whether something or someone is good for you

➢ Do you rush into your decisions? Do you decide in the moment without much thought? Sometimes this works, and sometimes it can land you in a heap of trouble. Do you ever create a self-imposed deadline to rush a decision or wait until the last minute so that the decision is rushed?

Do you trust yourself to make decisions?

➢ Do you make the decision and then keep doubting yourself? You did your homework, and the decision seemed right at the time. But when it comes to taking action, do you start doubting yourself and wondering if you are doing the right thing? Do you rarely take action? This is the most common complaint I get from my clients who are stuck. When you tell friends or colleagues and they reflect doubt also, do you allow the doubt to influence your decision?

➢ Do you wait to see what everybody else is doing? This is different from asking others' opinions in that you put everyone else first. Do you spend a lot of time waiting or wondering when it is going to be your turn?

➢ Do you wait until the worst happens before making a decision? Your back has been hurting for weeks, and you still haven't gone to the doctor. You won't go until your back has given out completely, even though you know it is going to take longer to heal. You may be getting clear clues that your company is closing down, but you wait until it closes before you start looking for a new job. You know a stair step is broken, and you decide not to fix it until someone is hurt. This is a typical decision-making route; most safety regulations are put in place after an accident happens.

➤ Do you avoid making decisions? Do you decide not to make a decision? Choosing not to decide is a decision. It may be as simple as you not having enough information, or the time may not be right. Your options may not feel right for you to decide, or you may be stuck and can't or won't decide.

➤ Do you like to keep your options open? Do you feel you need to keep so many doors open that to move in any direction is an achievement? This can work well while you explore the options until you discern the one for you. You may fear commitment, or your decision is not imminent. Your decision is to keep your options open.

➤ Do you look for permission? Do you ask your friends, family, and work colleagues to tell you what you should do? Maybe you don't know what you want, or you are used to others choosing for you. You prefer to have someone tell you what to

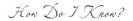

do so that you don't have to take responsibility for your decision.

➢ Do you make decisions according to your beliefs, regardless of the information available? We all do this. Beliefs define what or how we think, so they profoundly affect our decision-making process. If a belief means that things have to be a certain way, then the decision is made in a way that supports the "truth" of that belief. That's why I said earlier that what's true for you is not necessarily true for me. Trouble starts when we believe everybody must see it our way or when we try to make others see it our way. Trouble continues when decisions are made based on what is true for others and not you.

Are your decisions instinctive?

➢ Do you go by your gut instinct? My last realtor described this beautifully when she said, "I know without knowing how I know; I know because I know. When I decide from that knowing, I am always right." This works well when you are clear mentally and emotionally. The logic may or may not be relevant.

> ➤ Do you meditate? Do you sit in silence and wait for inspiration from within about what to choose?

Finally, do you use a combination of the above? What's your combination? Do you deliberate for weeks and then decide not to decide? Or do you make a decision based on love and then doubt yourself? Or do you take the logical route and ignore your gut instinct? Do you feel the fear and decide to take action anyway?

You may find that you use many of the decision-making methods, depending on the type of decision you are making. There are many ways to make decisions; these are the ways we are all familiar with.

When you know what type of decision maker you are, you can use the information in this book to do the following:

- Identify where you are making decisions from habitual patterns.
- Learn to use body/emotion signs and signals to realign your inner instincts with your logic and available information.
- Strengthen existing decision-making skills, developing your unique sense of what works best for you.

- Open to new decision making skills that support your goal and not your habits.

Our intellectual ability shows up in our grades. Did you know that we also have emotional and physical intelligence? And that the subconscious mind has more impact on our decisions than we realize? In the next few chapters, I will introduce you to these other intelligences and explain how they can influence your decisions and how some of the methods above can hijack your decision-making process.

Chapter Four

The Five Key Elements of Decision Making

The idea that decision making has five elements may make it sound complicated. But the five elements can help you understand how including your body wisdom can make the decision-making process much easier.

As you learn how to tune in to your inner wisdom and to combine that with what you already know, you can develop a simple decision-making technique based on the alignment of your mental intelligence (your IQ) and your emotional intelligence (your EQ). Once you decide, your thoughts, emotions, and body will be on the same page, and all your energy will align to support the action you choose.

It is much easier to take action when all is aligned than to take action when you are unsure that you are doing the right thing. The conflict that results can keep you from doing anything at all, cause you to constantly second-guess yourself, and make you wonder if you are missing something.

The five elements to consider when making decisions are

1. The mind's conscious thoughts and beliefs,
2. The mind's unconscious thoughts and beliefs,
3. The emotions,
4. The physical senses, and
5. The spiritual laws.

When all five elements are aligned, you feel comfortable about your decision, and the action to be taken feels like the most natural next step. When the five aspects are in conflict, you may experience doubt and procrastinate as you are overwhelmed and experience difficulty deciding to step in any direction.

1. The Mind's Conscious Thoughts and Beliefs

A belief is a thought process you buy into. Technically, the thought comes first. However, most of our beliefs (especially subconscious ones) lead us to think a certain way without questioning the truth of that belief. So in the following system, technically agreement with a thought leads to a belief. The converse is also true: the belief system leads us to think in a particular way.

We learned through our parents, caregivers, teachers, preachers, and others how to process information and use it to make decisions. To put it simply, we learned to make decisions based on what we believe and how we feel about that belief. Not only have we taken in a lot of information, we also have learned how to give meaning to what we learned. We have learned

- thoughts and how we should and shouldn't think;
- beliefs and what we should and shouldn't believe;
- feelings and how we should and shouldn't feel;
- meanings and what things mean or don't mean
- actions and how we should and shouldn't act.

Many teachings have been passed down through the generations, and most are wise. While your ancestors have many nuggets of wisdom to pass down, you have also inherited a vast number of fear-based beliefs or limited thoughts, feelings, and so on.

The main use of intelligence is to gather known information from your resources and to use that to make clear decisions about your life and relationships. You can also learn from experience. This is the most valuable learning, and it can run into a sticky wicket when your experience contradicts social norm. You may already see that relying on intellect alone may be tricky in many circumstances, especially in big life decisions. Making decisions relying on this limited external information alone can be even trickier.

We don't have to reinvent the wheel, and we certainly can stand on the shoulders of what our ancestors learned and use the information from things that worked. But making a decision today based on tradition or past family ways of doing things can be misleading and can have no relevance to what you are deciding on today.

2. The Minds Unconscious Thoughts and Beliefs

While all the other aspects of decision making can influence the process, this aspect is the one that might trip you up the most. Your subconscious mind works 24/7. It holds the memory of every thought, word, action, feeling, sight, sense, and smell of every happening in your life. It has been referred to as the emotional mind, and many refer to the subconscious mind as the body.

When you learn to do something new like driving, playing golf, or riding a bike, there are many things to remember at first. For example, in golf, you must remember many details to develop the perfect swing. Over time, with repeated practice, the subconscious mind takes over so you don't have to be conscious of every movement or action. This is how we develop habits, good or bad.

The subconscious is also where you store deep-seated beliefs about yourself and about how you need to be. All positive and negative experiences are stored there. Some of your old beliefs and experiences may be long forgotten, and you may disagree with them now. However, the belief with the strongest emotional charge produces the results in your life. You may set a goal to lose weight, for example. You do everything you know to reduce your weight, to cut your calorie intake, to exercise, and to eat healthy foods. If you have an underlying belief that says, "I was born to be overweight," your subconscious will bypass your new habits and continue to create or sustain fat cells in your body. The result may be that no matter what you try, you will not lose the weight you want to lose.

If you grew up hearing, "No one in our family ever amounted to anything," and you believe it, you will find it very difficult to amount to anything. If you believe you are unlovable, you will have great difficulty finding a partner who will love you. It won't be that he or she doesn't love you; it will be that you won't be able to accept that love. Why? Because you have subconscious beliefs, emotions, and attachments that support your supposed *unlovability*.

I guarantee you that if there is something happening in your life that you don't like or want, there is a subconscious belief, agreement, or emotional memory that creates it. Apparently 93 percent of our thoughts are subconscious. So old beliefs, commitments, agreements, or memories can keep the undesirable result in your life.

3. Emotions in Decision Making

Emotions are a direct response to your thoughts, not to the world around you.

This idea may be new to you, but it is true just the same. Emotions are energy moving in the body and are a direct response to the thought you are thinking. So, when you think a thought, you trigger a chemical response in your brain. This creates senses in your body. These senses combine to create emotions.

In truth, emotion is evidence of whether you, as a whole—that is, your mind, body, and spirit—are in harmony or aligned with the thought you are thinking or not. In general, if you feel positive emotions, you are aligned with or in agreement with the thought, and if you are not aligned, you feel negative emotions.

The role of emotions in the decision-making process has been confused over the years. Often we have learned to use emotions as the reason or to justify a particular decision or action: I did this because I loved him. I was angry, so I couldn't help myself. The key point here is that while emotions are very real, they are not necessarily a true reflection of what is going on. They are messengers reflecting our response to the thought. The brain does not know the difference between real or imagined thought, so we need to regard emotions as information, not as fact.

The effects of positive emotions (such as love and joy) and negative emotions (such as anger and fear) are very evident in our decisions. In other words, you will make a different decision when angry than you will when in love. We all have emotions, and the meanings we attribute to emotions are relative to the individual rather than the truth.

4. The Physical Senses Response in Decision Making

We are highly intelligent beings with a sensory mechanism designed to complement our decision-making process. The body is a genius sensory being, and it responds to thoughts. Where and how you feel this sense can be a powerful assistant to your decision-making process.

As I said previously, emotions are energy moving through your body. When you have a thought that disrupts your flow of energy, your body lets you know in the form of a sense of discomfort or dis-ease. The body feels at ease when in alignment or agreement with the thought. Tensing and dis-ease indicate disharmony.

Have you noticed that you tend to move away from things you don't like and move closer to things you do like? Would you believe that unicellular organisms do the same in a very simple way? Inside your body, your cells actually contract when exposed to toxins and expand when nutrients are present. To keep it simple, you can relate a sense to the function of that particular part of the body. So the best decisions are made when at ease; ease indicates that the thoughts and emotions and body are all on the same page, or aligned.

Many books and references act as a guide to what the senses may mean for individuals. In my experience, what you feel and where is unique to you, based on your take on what you have learned during your life. For example, the back is often associated with support, as the skeleton supports your whole structure. We have expressions like "a monkey on your back" to indicate stresses a person carries. Lower back pain can indicate you are backing out on yourself, not supporting yourself. Shoulder pain can indicate that emotional support is required; you need a shoulder to lean on. Do any of these sound familiar to you?

5. The Spiritual Laws in Decision Making

Spiritual laws are exact. The universe provides mirrors for us to look in.

Our world is governed by many different laws. Human laws were made to keep us safe in the community. The laws of physics describe gravity, energy, and now quantum physics, determining the nature of possibilities. There are also spiritual laws, also called the natural laws of the universe. These are described in ancient spiritual texts like the Bible, Koran, Celtic scripts, etc. In more recent times, you may have heard of the law of attraction and the laws of abundance and prosperity. These are well known and documented, and they describe our relationships with our world. You may also have heard the terms "as above so below" or "as without, so within." In spiritual law, our outside world is a reflection of what is within. A conflict in your life is a reflection of a conflict within you.

In decision-making, these laws can be useful. According to the law of attraction, for example, you are like a magnet attracting people and situations that resonate with your energy vibration. So when people say you are on their wavelength, well, you are. You are always in the process of attracting something or someone into your life. Your energy field is created by your thoughts and feelings, and the universe acts like a mirror, sending back a reflection of the energy you are projecting.

How is this useful in decision making? If you like what you are attracting, keep doing what you are doing. If you don't like what you are attracting, change what you attract by observing your results and reconsidering your decisions to create different outcomes.

Have you ever said to yourself, "I can't understand why he/she is in my life? He /she is so negative and nothing like I am." The more you deny that you are a magnet for a type of person or situation, the tougher it gets. To really take charge, look at and address the balance of that quality in yourself. (Or you will keep attracting the old scenarios!)

So your decision process has five elements in two parts: (1) the inner part, which is unconscious thoughts, gut instinct (bodily feelings), and emotions; and (2) the outer part, which is conscious thoughts (existing knowledge, information on the Internet, beliefs, and so on) and the use of natural or spiritual laws. In the next section, we will explore how the five elements can trip up your decisions despite your best efforts and affect your life as a result.

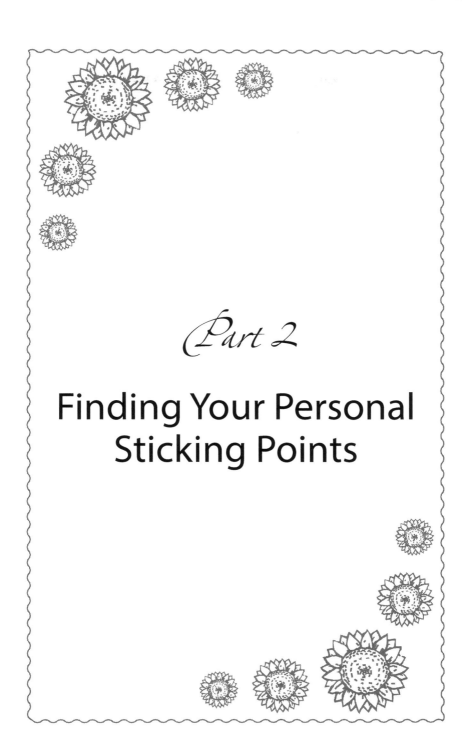

Part 2

Finding Your Personal Sticking Points

Chapter Five

The Mind Element— Thoughts

> If you believe you can or if you believe you can't, you are right.
> Henry Ford

Do Your Beliefs Cause You to Make Decisions That Hurt You?

So how can beliefs become sticking points when you are making decisions? Beliefs are made up of thoughts and words you agree with. While a lot of your beliefs support you, many of your beliefs were designed to protect you and are fear based, so they limit you in some way. Many of your beliefs may have worked well when you were a child, but as you grow older, you may find many limiting beliefs that need to be reworked.

Let's face it: limiting beliefs set in childhood rarely have relevance in your life today. Or do they? For simplicity, and to show how beliefs affect decisions, I have divided beliefs into four categories. This chapter refers mainly to limiting beliefs.

1. *Programmed beliefs.* These are ideas and beliefs we learned over the years from our families, friends, schools, and the media. Mostly your beliefs have been formed to support you. Fear-based beliefs were designed to protect you and keep you safe by limiting you in some way.

2. *Trauma.* We form beliefs when we experience trauma. This could be a genuine trauma, like an accident or a scary or embarrassing incident. Our decision after experiencing a trauma or something unpleasant is usually something like "I am never doing that again."

3. *Non-traumatic experience.* You interacted with your world from day one, and everything you learned from others you incorporated into your own interpretation of what it meant to you. You decided what to believe based on your personal experience. This differs from trauma in that the information is created without a traumatic event.

4. *Word associations.* Words and your relationships to them are important, as words create your thoughts. Your associations with words and the meanings you give them can differ from those experienced by other people, and this in turn can influence your beliefs and their impact on your life.

Current studies claim that roughly 90 to 93 percent of our thoughts are subconscious. Yes, you read correctly. A vast majority of your thought process is not in your awareness, while only 7 to 10 percent of your thoughts are conscious. It is also thought that most of our beliefs are formed before we reach seven years of age.

But how do you form beliefs? Limiting beliefs are formed initially to protect you. They are called limiting because they limit you in some aspect of your life and are fear based. So, based on the statistics above, you can imagine how many limited beliefs are running under your radar. Sometimes you are told what to believe, and you may have had to accept what you were told.

You are not wired to remember every single thing you have heard or every thought you have had, and all your beliefs are stored in your subconscious mind. What you decide to believe at age five, you will no longer believe at twenty-five. However, if you have a strong feeling about the decision you made as a five-year-old, it may still be playing out in your life today. Check it out. Is an early belief still affecting your life?

We each have a unique perspective on life. We create this by having a thought about what is happening and a corresponding feeling about that thought. The nature of the feeling usually determines whether we do or don't like what is going on. If we have a positive feeling, there is a good chance we like what is happening, and if we have a negative feeling it is likely we don't like what is happening. This determines our decision-making process. We rarely make a decision to take action to do something we know is going to make us feel bad—not purposefully, at any rate.

For example, you are not going to order what you least like for dinner or buy clothes that don't suit you. Nor would you date someone you don't like or apply for a job you are not qualified for. In general, you make decisions to remain in your comfort zone or to go in the direction that takes you where you want to go.

So how do beliefs influence your decision-making process?

You See Your Life through a Filter of the Beliefs

You perceive situations through your belief system. If the belief is challenged, you may want to defend it. Any time you hear yourself saying, "I have to," "I should," "I must," or "It has always been this way," explore the possibility of a limiting belief lurking just beneath the surface of your awareness.

Have you heard of self-fulfilling prophecies? How many times have you told yourself, "I knew that would happen" or "I had a funny feeling about that." Over time, we learn to use our feelings and experiences to confirm our beliefs. The belief/emotion (energy) combination creates an expectation of what will happen based on the belief of it happening that way. This can go both ways. You create your dream life if you believe you can, just as you create your life to be as *hard* as you believe it needs to be.

For example, you may have been reprimanded in school for speaking up at a tender age and made a decision that speaking up is dangerous. You may experience a lot of situations in your adult life where you needed to speak up, but because the belief is still running the show, you decide that it is unsafe, so you don't say anything. As an adult, you make up excuses to justify not speaking up, like "I don't want to hurt their feelings" or "They don't need to hear that now" or "I'll be fired if I say that." Often fear of speaking up can be reflected in throat problems.

You decide based on the filter/perception and not on what is really happening.

The Corresponding Emotion (Fear)
Makes a Belief Seem Real

The danger with limiting beliefs when making a decision is that often they are subconscious. Your fear response to a thought is immediate and so real it is hard to tell that what feels very real is not necessarily true. You use your feelings to prove or to add value to what you think: "It must be true, because I am feeling this way." In reality, the senses making up the emotion may mean something else entirely.

You decisions can be completely misguided when you mistake the belief as being a fact and use the emotion to back it up.

You May Be Inclined to Think
Your Beliefs Are You

Have you ever heard yourself saying, "This is how I always do it" or "This is who I am"? The deeper the belief the more you will be identified with it as being you.

Your decisions are based on who you think you are— according to your belief and not according to your authentic self.

When a Belief Is to Suffer, It Becomes More
Important Than the Desired Result

A belief acts as an attachment or limit. Do you believe in hard work and therefore set up situations where work is hard? (Even though you love your job)

Another belief is "No pain, no gain." So people go for exercise programs that are excruciating. (You may have you seen evidence of this on TV.) If you believe you need to suffer, you will.

Your decisions will tend to support suffering consciously and unconsciously. It is possible that you won't see the option to do things in a way that works for you. You will naturally rule out opportunities.

We Gather Information to Support Our Beliefs until They Are "Fact" to Us.

This is an interesting pitfall, because when we mistake beliefs for facts, our decision process can be based on "facts" that have no basis in truth and distract us from what we really want to achieve.

I had an interesting discussion with a colleague recently. She had a belief that directly opposed mine. She believed, like many, that Friday the thirteenth is an unlucky day, that bad things always happened on this date. She had a list as long as her arm of all the things that had gone wrong for her on those Fridays. She believed this to the point that she rarely arranged to do anything or meet anyone on that date, unless she absolutely had to.

We had arranged to play in a golf tournament on a Friday the thirteenth, and she wasn't looking forward to it. All the way to the golf course, she complained that it was Friday the thirteenth and that she would probably play terribly. I told her my view: thirteen is a number of mastery, and Friday the thirteenth is the day that I focus on doing things to the best of my ability. So I was expecting to play well because, for me, it was a day for doing what I do well.

You won't believe what happened. We were divided into different groups, and the group who had the best score won. My colleague told me excitedly after the tournament that she had gotten a hole in one, and her team had won a prize. She was delighted, and as she went off to change, she said, "Who would have thought? On Friday the thirteenth, of all days." That day she decided that she was going to think of Friday the thirteenth differently.

Mistaking belief for fact can dramatically affect your decisions to support the belief, ignoring the facts.

Your Beliefs Keep You from Listening to Other Points of View

Having preconceived ideas can stop us from seeing the big picture and can lead us to make decisions to fit the preconceived idea. We have learned to relate and compare everything to something familiar, so that we can identify with it—that is, maintain the comfort zone of knowing. For example, when I tell some people I am a coach, they immediately relate this to counseling. Often this is because they don't relate to or understand coaching. I usually have a tough job telling them otherwise. They don't hear me through the filter of the preconception and fit everything I say into what they know about counselors.

I have a friend who is a police officer, and he agrees. He said different people see, hear, and express their version of the crime scene based on their unique perspective. That's why the police get as many accounts of an incident as possible to improve their chances of getting the whole story. It makes sense.

A belief acts as a preconceived idea. Once we agree with a thought and the associated words, a decision becomes predetermined also; it is made to agree with the belief. You might be thinking, *Isn't there only one reality?* There may be only one reality, but there are many perceptions of that reality. Do you know anybody who can recount the same story in many ways? I have a friend who tells a story differently depending on her mood, and I have learned not to trust her version of events.

When we see, hear, speak, relate, and act through our beliefs, it sometimes rules out a two-way conversation. And decisions are biased to the belief in every way. Most people constantly look for evidence to support their belief through others' words, actions, and behavior.

Why do our beliefs seem so real?

The mind aspect of the decision-making process includes thoughts and words that make up the beliefs. The thoughts generate the feelings. The feelings in turn generate more thoughts that support the belief, which in turn generates more feelings. So it is easy to believe that the belief is real, as the feelings appear to support it. Everybody else does it this way, right? The resultant decision really *feels* like it's the right one for you. And on that note, have you ever noticed how you can talk yourself into doing something as easily as talking yourself out of doing something?

Here's an example: Jane was feeling down. Her friend Tony had gone out without her, and she felt left out. The more she thought about it, the worse she felt. Later that evening, another friend called, and they spoke about a completely different topic. Jane's thought process changed, and the sad feelings disappeared. Have you ever experienced this? Or a particular subject comes up that makes you uncomfortable, so you choose to change the subject to avoid the discomfort. This is natural, and you can see how the decision you make may change, depending on how you feel.

We Learned to Rate Outside Opinions as being More Important Than Our Own

As schoolchildren, we presented our work to a teacher in the format the teacher wanted. We did what we were told at home. We learned to behave a certain way to make people happy, and we learned the behaviors that didn't make people happy. As soon as I learned that the teacher didn't want my opinion, but rather an "educated" opinion, my grades improved dramatically. All the systems in society are useful because they define a safe structure within which we are safe.

When you make decisions based on outside opinions rather than your own, on one hand you take in a broader perspective, but on the other, you may limit yourself to what works for them and not you.

Limiting Beliefs Can Prevent Us from Recognizing Opportunities

Can you see how limited beliefs can interfere with the decision-making process? The emphasis moves from what you really want to what you think you want or what you learned you want. Is it any wonder we might feel unfulfilled? As your beliefs shape your reality, you may have an opportunity staring you in the face, but you may not recognize it because you can't see it as such. For example, even Prince Charming looks like a jerk through the "every guy I meet is a jerk" filter. The reverse is also true. Jerks can appear to be like Prince Charming when you look through the "I deserve to be disrespected" filter.

Your decisions are made accordingly.

A Lot of Our Goals Have Been Set by Others

This occurred through well-intentioned teaching, which I call conditioning or programming. In the coaching process, I help people explore their goals, filtering out ones that no longer work for them.

Beliefs with the Strongest Emotional Charge Bring the Results

A limiting belief shows up in your life as evidence of a gap between your circumstances at present and where you want to be instead. That gap usually presents as a conflict of some sort. You may not be achieving your goals; you may be attracting the same jerk; you find it impossible to lose that weight; you are passed over for that promotion again.

One of my clients was single and really wanted to be married. She wanted a deeply loving partner and wasn't prepared to settle. She was doing all the things necessary to meet people. But she couldn't understand what was keeping Mr. Right from coming into her life. On the surface, she was telling herself that she really wanted to meet someone, but a deep belief she had about herself was that she was not worthy of deep love from someone she cared about. The conscious thought and the unconscious belief were directly conflicted, which is like having a foot on the gas and a foot on the brake at the same time. And the thought process (belief) with the strongest emotional charge won out. Once she reprogrammed her subconscious belief, Mr. Right turned up in her life quickly.

> A belief is true only as long as
> we believe it to be so.
> You arrange your life and results
> to support that "truth."
> You *can* change your mind about a
> belief and with that your reality.

Making clear decisions about what you want and setting goals to bring about what you want are based on a clear understanding of how beliefs influence your decisions.

What can you do about this?

What Is the Difference Between a Supporting Belief and a Limiting Belief?

The former supports us, and the latter restricts us in some way. Supporting beliefs are those we can grow with. We have many supporting beliefs, such as "treat others as you would like to be treated" and "live and let live." They allow us to grow and don't limit us in any way. The predominant emotion behind supporting beliefs is love.

Understanding that our limiting beliefs are usually fear based is a key to the process of freeing ourselves of those beliefs. It's also important to understand the universal law of reflection: The world outside of me reflects the world within (see chapter 9, "The Great Unknown"). If there is a conflict or disharmony in my outer world, it is a reflection of a conflict within.

A number of indicators, mostly behavioral, can alert you to limiting beliefs. I will cover the two main ones here: we defend to protect our belief or we attack an offender to protect our belief. (I am deliberately exaggerating here.) The intensity of your response is directly proportional to the depth of your belief. In other words, if your belief is intense, you will be in the stress zone, which is designed for quick defensive strategies, not logical problem solving. Fear and anger will be the predominant emotions.

1. **Defensive Strategies**

   By far the most common strategy is to defend your position. Do you find yourself saying things like "But you don't understand," "I'm hurt that you don't agree with me," "Let me explain why my way is best," "Why can't you listen to me?" and so on. We have many defense strategies, because our definition of what is true is deeply rooted. To defend, we must perceive we are being threatened or attacked. *Note:* Each limiting belief may have a number of limiting beliefs supporting it. It is linked with underlying emotions and one or more linked behaviors.

2. **Judgment Strategies**

   Judgment follows hot on the heels of defense. It is a way to protect your belief by blaming or making the other wrong in his or her belief. Of course this means that you are right (whether you are or not doesn't matter). You may say things like "You can't possibly believe that," "But that is crazy," or "Let me tell you how wrong you are."

These reactions are on opposite ends of a scale of potential reactions. You probably know your particular variety of reaction. Whatever it is, it usually reinforces your beliefs and opinions, validating or justifying your behavior and deepening the patterns that may be holding you from the changes that could break through those glass ceilings once and for all. (Glass ceilings are places where you are stuck and you have no idea why. They are called glass ceilings because you can see clearly what you want to achieve, but you can't see what is stopping you. Another term used to describe this is *blind spot*.)

Most importantly, both defense and judgment stem from fear and can stop you from realizing what you want.

How Do I Know That Changing the Belief Will Change My Reality?

At a very basic level, changing your belief changes your thought processes from the inside out. Your brain gets a different instruction, which creates a different biochemical response. You emotional response also changes, and the decisions you make and the subsequent actions are different as a result. Don't forget how each belief has strings attached in the form of thoughts, physical feelings, emotions, and behaviors. Becoming aware of a limiting belief is the first step. Addressing the emotional energy that is often the glue that holds the belief in place changes the energy. For example, you change a belief based on fear to a belief based on joy. Simply put, you stop believing, and you allow yourself a change of mind. Your decision process changes as a result.

How Will I Know a Limiting Belief Has Been Activated?

The fear that was the basis of the underlying limiting belief will show up in many guises. How does it show up for you? Do you procrastinate? Become overwhelmed? Make excuses about being busy? Decide it's not for you? Judge it as not being good enough? Blame someone or something? Find you are taking things personally?

The fear protects you by preventing you from taking that risk again. You find yourself saying, "You see, I told you that would happen." And the funny thing is, if you don't say it yourself, you'll find that you attract someone who will. The fear holding that belief in place, to keep you safe, keeps you from taking action.

Or it shows up when you tell friends or loved ones that you are contemplating a change and their reaction is "Are you crazy?' or "What do you want to do that for?" or "Aren't you happy here?" If what they say stops you, you may want to explore the possibility that a limiting belief is holding you.

It is important to note that many beliefs can contribute to a particular behavior and to how we make our decisions. What if you had a belief that you aren't good enough? This would lead you to behave in a particular way. Maybe you don't challenge yourself, or you constantly criticize yourself, or you find you are friends with critical people. There will be a number of beliefs behind this. You may believe you are not good-looking enough; someone made a passed remark that you overheard when you were a child, and you thought she must know what she was talking about—so you believed her. You may believe you are not smart enough. You may believe many negative things, and as a result you don't try new things or new relationships.

You can decide to believe something different through awareness and understanding, but if the emotional charge of the old pattern or belief still holds you, the actions and therefore results will turn out the same. In other words, if the new belief tries to set foundations on the old charge, there will be no lasting change. I have met many people who said they spent years in talk therapy, and while they fully understood their issue, they still had a lot of emotional energy around it. They were still triggered by similar events.

A combination of emotional freedom techniques, energy methods, and the talk process can help you make huge inroads in releasing or embracing your old patterns. Will power alone won't work. Conversely, you can release the emotional charge, but over time the belief and the thought process can reactivate the emotional response. And as for the behavior—it continues! *Bottom line, in my experience, addressing both the thought and the emotion is the most effective way to change an old belief.*

How Can I Change an Old, Limiting Belief?

Questioning the truth of the belief is a good start. Remember, a belief is a thought you agree with. And while it may have been true at one time, that may no longer be the case. Giving yourself permission to change your mind opens the potential for more possibilities— particularly the possibility of choice. I invite you to explore a different avenue.

- Identify the beliefs you are most attached to. These are usually the beliefs that you most passionately defend, and you use them to stay the same even when you know it is time to step out of your comfort zone. Releasing attachments occurs by changing the thought and by changing the feeling and energy around the thought. A good example of this is when you discover something you once believed as a truth, is not actually true after all. Or maybe a new scientific discovery reveals a theory that causes you to rethink your belief system. After all, at one point in history, our belief was that the earth was flat.

- Ask the question, is this still true? Or do I really have to do things this way?
- Be open to other possibilities, options, and perspectives.
- Notice your feelings. Do you feel restricted or at ease when you think about the belief. And more importantly, notice your feelings if you think about changing that belief.

Often just realizing that the belief is no longer true changes everything. And you become open to seeing situations from a different perspective. Knowing that there are many different opinions and perspectives out there can help you get perspective on your opinion also.

The beauty is you can always change your mind. Changing how you feel about that old belief (See chapter 7 on emotions.) is how a belief is neutralized, and you become free to make a new decision about what you want instead. You will find yourself saying things like "I didn't realize how much that old belief has been affecting my life." The reward is simple. You begin to open up to the possibilities that were always there, but that you couldn't see through that old belief filter. "It has to be done this way" becomes "There are a number of ways you can approach this." "There is no way out" becomes "There is always another way."

It can be useful to remember that beliefs are thoughts we have attached to by agreeing with them. Often your learned beliefs just need a little tweaking to restore a balance or perspective that works better for you. And at other times they can be discarded altogether. Sometimes it is not so much the belief but our relationship to that belief that determines our reality. So when you find yourself saying, "I believe this because …," what meaning have you placed on the belief? Or do you believe it because you are afraid not to?

Chapter Six

The Power of Words.

$\mathcal{M}$uch like beliefs, our relationship with words limits our decision-making process, since words make up the beliefs in the first place. The meanings put on words differ greatly. Those meanings are based on our experiences growing up. Look back to what you learned from your parents. What is happening in your life today? Can you see similarities?

It is amazing how many ways the same word can be interpreted. For example, *respect* may mean something entirely different to each person in a relationship. It would be well worth your while to ask a prospective partner how he or she interprets certain words. You will be able to establish very quickly if you are on the same page or not.

Let's look at a few more words to give you an idea of what I mean. The word *commitment* can mean an obligation or entrapment to some and freedom to others. We all know people who are afraid to commit because they don't want to be tied down. *Responsibility* is seen by some as liability or as a reason for blame. Others see responsibility as an honor and a challenge.

How does this affect decisions? If you interpret *commitment* as an obligation, you may fear it and avoid making the decisions that mean commitment. You may find decisions around the word *responsibility* difficult also.

We can have a lot of energy or emotional charge around a word. A great example is the word *no.* Think back to when you were young. How did you respond when you heard the word *no*? Do you respond differently now? Ask yourself the following questions:

- Was hearing the word *no* a positive or negative experience?
- Does your association with the word *no* keep you from asking for help?
- Does it stop you from asking for anything at all?
- Does it motivate you to rebel?

- Do you feel strong emotion when told *no*?
- When you hear the word *no*, do you take it personally?
- Do you have positive associations with the word *no*?
- Do you see it as an aid to creating healthy boundaries as a parent, partner, or colleague?
- Do you see it as a way to stop going in a particular direction and to refocus your energies to what will work more effectively?

No can be all those things; it depends on your relationship with it. Jenny, my client, got angry every time she heard the word *no*. For some reason she associated the word *no* with punishment; it meant that she was bad in some way. She knew she was overreacting by taking *no* personally and didn't know why. Her response was to rebel against the *no,* and often this ended up being to her detriment. As a result she didn't like to say no to anybody either.

It turned out she had a very strict upbringing and didn't like being told what not to do. This led to her developing a strong emotional charge related to the word *no*. When she released the emotional charge, she redefined *no* as the valuable asset that it truly is. Saying no to what doesn't work for you is really saying yes to self. *No* became a tool for Jenny to create healthy boundaries in her life, allowing her to stay focused on decisions and actions that led her to realizing her goals.

You can have emotional attachments to words that influence your decision-making process and the actions you do or don't take as a result.

One of my clients changed her career and moved into the healing work she loved. She moved from an intensely stressful job in medical sales before she burned out. However, she found that she created her new business in a way that naturally caused stress. That was not her intention, but she had spent so many years working in a way that stress practices, competition, and conflict motivated her that she found it difficult to do anything else. Her association with the word *work* was that it is stressful and difficult.

Her beliefs, decisions, and actions generated stress even though her new business was based on stress relief. Ironic! Her coaching involved exploring her associations and beliefs she held around the word *work*. She redefined all the beliefs she had formed through past experience and redefined *work* as a discipline that she could perform with relative ease. She basically broke her habitual work/ stress association and replaced it with ease instead.

Becoming aware of differing word associations may help you to uncover your own associations that block you from recreating your life in a way you want it.

Words Vibrate at Particular Energy Frequencies

The power of a word is important for another reason. Words, like musical notes, resonate at different frequencies. Studies have shown that each word has a vibration or energy frequency associated with it. The flowing and harmonious energy of *balance* has a higher frequency than *imbalance*. You can guess that words like *gratitude*, *success*, and *grace* have a higher frequency than words with negative connotations. When you start speaking more positively about yourself and others, you naturally raise your energy levels.

Have you ever noticed how your words can depress you? Or elate you? Or even create anger? You can tell if your energy is high or low through your emotions. Anger, sadness, and depression are examples of emotions that resonate at a low frequency, while love and joy are high frequency emotions.

When you raise your energy levels using kind words, you begin to create a different chemical response inside your body. You start to feel more at ease, and your body releases the tension created by fear. One of the best ways to turn around a thought process is to change the thought to gratitude or a better-feeling thought, as crazy as this may sound. Though you may not like the situation you are in, that change automatically raises the energy frequency and starts a chemical change inside your body. The more balanced you are in thought and emotion, the easier it is to make a clear decision that supports you. The more off balance you are—thinking negatively and creating a stress/adrenalin reaction in your body—the more likely you will make a decision that won't support you as well.

You can easily see this when pacifying a crying child. If you can distract her with something that makes her feel better, she stops crying and forgets about what offended her in the first place. In the same way, if you are thinking negatively, distracting yourself with a more positive thought will shift the negative feeling to one that feels better.

You can easily establish your associations with words, beliefs, and decisions. See the yes-or-no modal on page 110 and then do this exercise.

Word or Belief Assessment Exercise

1. Take a moment to say out loud a word or belief that comes to mind. (Use a word or belief that you feel strongly about. Stick with *no* if you prefer.)
2. Notice what you feel in your body.
3. Where are you feeling it?
4. Is there an emotion present?
5. Do you notice any memories coming up?

6. Grade the intensity of the feeling: 0 = ease; 10 = most tense.

This is a very simple exercise to develop your own scale of your relationships to thoughts beliefs or words. You can use it for assessing your decisions and how they flow with your system. Say your decision out loud. Notice what you feel in your body. Tension? Ease?

Take the exercise a step further.

1. Replace the words, belief, or decision with words that reflect what you want instead.
2. How does the feeling in your body change?
3. Write down your answer.

If you feel tension when you state what you want, it can be an indicator of underlying conflict in your subconscious. This is usually a signal of a belief that may be blocking your desire from coming about. It may be 'I am not worthy' or 'Its ok for them but not for me' or 'I am not allowed'. This can really help you identify beliefs that you are ready to reframe into a dynamic that works for you. You will begin to understand this as you explore your emotions in the next chapter.

Chapter Seven

Tuning in to Emotional States

The biggest challenge is learning how to use your emotions to inform your decision-making process and subsequent actions and not to define them. Emotions often confuse the decision process.

The Emotional Element of the Decision-Making Process

What are emotions anyway? Did you know that *emotion* means energy in motion in the body? E-motion. You were designed to let your emotions flow within. The trouble starts when you try to block your emotions.

You may do this for many reasons, but usually it is out of fear—the core emotion of stress. Why would you keep your emotions from flowing? Because you may not feel safe expressing them. Because you are not sure how to. Because you may not have been allowed to express your emotions, but were told, "Stop that crying," "Don't be angry with your brother," or "Don't be sad." Or because you were criticized, embarrassed, shamed, or made to feel guilty because of your emotions. You may be afraid of what others may think.

So your natural tendency might be to try not to feel. The emotion may create an overwhelming feeling in your body, and you didn't learn what to do with that. Emotions fluster the thought process also, and when you are in a state of strong emotion, it becomes difficult to decide what to do next. So it can be difficult to take action in the moment.

These feelings and fears are our teachers. And would you believe that connecting with them and getting to know them is at the core of how we learn to trust ourselves completely? We can use them to support our decision-making process instead of letting them cloud it.

As I said earlier, emotions are energy that can be compared to the light spectrum. They form a band of frequencies moving from fear right through to joy. Fear is the lowest frequency vibration, and joy, love, and gratitude are the highest. Obviously the higher the frequency, the better you feel. You can recognize this through a feeling of ease throughout your body. And fear can feel uneasy or tense. (Think of the startle reflex; your whole body freezes.) Each emotion feels differently in your body.

Your emotional frequencies emanate from you and determine what you attract into your life. For example, if you want to attract a loving partner and experience low self esteem, your vibrational energy is more likely to attract someone who will reinforce your low self-esteem. On another note, you may want more money but support a 'lack' mentality, constantly feeling you don't have enough. Putting all your focus on low frequency thoughts, i.e. 'I don't have enough', cancels out what you really want and the most likely result is that you won't have enough money. The thought with the most energy creates the result.

I coach executives on how to play their 'A' Game under pressure, through managing stress. In my experience, the number-one cause of stress is arguing with reality. I have worked with thousands and found that, while we all have a sensory system, each individual has his own unique emotional intelligence system based on how he learned to feel about his thoughts (beliefs).

A large part of my work with clients is helping them develop their emotional intelligence. Emotional intelligence is not just about acknowledging the emotions you feel, it is about knowing what emotions are and how to deal with them. For example, I learned to associate spiders with my fear response, so every time I see a spider I react with fear, whether the spider is poisonous or not. The truth is that we have learned to misinterpret our emotions.

Developing emotional intelligence is like learning a foreign language. You learn by relating the new words to your existing language. In emotional intelligence, you learn how to connect your words and thoughts to the emotions and the senses in your body. You develop a language that allows you to fully understand yourself. Knowing that ease means agreement and tension means conflict, you begin to develop guidelines that relate to your likes and dislikes, based on your inner compass, rather than depending on hearsay or the opinions of others.

This skill set can be learned, and the more you practice, the more you will experience being true to you. *Emotional intelligence* is a term used to define how you interpret and use your emotions effectively. Also emotions need to be released once you have received your inner information about whatever you are thinking. Just as our body removes excess water and food, we need to release excess emotional energy. I call this emotional hygiene.

How Do Emotions Affect Your Decision-Making Process?

We have learned to believe emotions are true. Did you know that feelings are a direct response to your thought *about* what is happening in your world. For example, if you have a preprogrammed thought or belief, you also have a preprogrammed emotion corresponding to that thought or belief. The trouble is, the brain doesn't know the difference between real and imagined. It does what it is told or taught to do.

You know how you can get upset about something just by thinking about it? You may get annoyed when someone drives into your parking space or eats the cupcake you were saving. Those emotions and subtle senses are as a result of the thought telling the brain what to do. Yes, the senses are how emotions are felt in the body.

This affects your decision-making process because it is easy to mistake the old preprogrammed emotion as true. Now, I can understand how this can be confusing. But earlier I told you there are five main elements to the decision-making process: conscious mind thoughts and beliefs, unconscious mind thoughts and beliefs, emotions, physical senses, and spiritual laws. If your preprogrammed thoughts create preprogrammed emotions, you have to question your emotions as well as your thoughts. Are they really true? Don't get me wrong; the feelings are real. But the reasons we attribute to them may not be truth.

Have you ever been afraid, such as when thinking of doing a driving test or making a presentation? What happens? Do the fear or the nerves impede your process? Do you perform as well as you would like? In my experience and that of my clients, fear impairs performance. You see this in sports also. It is important to keep calm, as the adrenalin surge caused by fear can affect performance by interfering—with the balance of the swing in golf, for example.

We Often Fear Fear Itself and Other Emotions, Like Anger

Emotional intelligence is the one area most of us like to avoid if at all possible, especially the "negative" emotions. As you have seen in the past few chapters, there are more ways to hide from fear than there are people on the planet. And there are just as many ways to avoid conflict or create it.

The human race hasn't learned how to deal with emotions very well. We just don't know what to do with them. As a result, we are afraid of them. For generations there have been acceptable and unacceptable ways of dealing with emotions, especially "negative" emotions. *Acceptable* has usually meant suppressing, repressing, depressing, withholding, and hiding the feeling while you express a grievance with as little emotion as possible, if you express it at all. We also learned how to express positive feelings in an "acceptable" way. *Unacceptable* has meant expressing negative emotions through physical demonstrations, such as shouting, crying, or arguing. There is a sliding scale between these two. Both are ways to hide from the discomfort of the feelings, instead of feeling them according to our design.

This can get tricky when we make decisions. We tend to judge emotions to be right or wrong and sometimes judge others as good or bad. We also wonder what others will think. Often decisions are made to avoid expressing anger or to prevent a confrontation. What happens if you really need to deliver a message? Do emotions stop you? Or do emotions drive your decision to act? It is difficult to make the same decision when angry that you would make when calm and collected.

Trying Something New

Unfortunately, these moments of strong emotion come up most frequently when we are reaching for big goals or when we are trying to implement change. Whether you want to make more money, further your career, grow a business, go for that relationship, or improve your fitness, strong emotions are involved. Any time you go for gold, try to play big, and get what you want, emotions come up—especially fear. As a result, you are working with only a fraction of your intelligence. So it goes without saying that you are also tapping into a fraction of your potential.

This affects your decision-making process. Fear can cause you to avoid trying new things and/or avoid taking those steps that lead to success. How scary is it to ask someone new out, for example? It is important to note that we are programmed to trigger fear as a go-to position when facing a new experience. This makes sense, as it motivates us to proceed with caution; we should not let fear stop us altogether, which is what happens so often.

Old Events and the Associated Emotions Can Mask What Is Happening Now

New evidence shows how our brain processes challenging emotional events like trauma. Any time you experience a trauma, everything in that moment—the sight, the sounds, the smells, and the way you feel—are downloaded into your subconscious mind as a trigger. It's as if there is a big sign in your memory saying, "Avoid anything like this in the future." The thing is, the subconscious doesn't distinguish between a major accident or trauma and a less challenging event.

A colleague described how he spent a large part of his young life in the hospital. As a result of this trauma, he did not go near hospitals or doctors unless he absolutely had to. The emotional charge he held in his conscious and subconscious dictated his decisions about visiting a doctor or having anything to do with hospitals for a long time.

Here's another great example. You are in first grade. Your teacher is talking to the class, and you interrupt with a question. The teacher yells at you, "Be quiet! Never interrupt while I am talking." You feel terrified and humiliated. From then on, every time you are about to ask a question of someone of authority, that trigger is reactivated. You feel the same feelings of terror and humiliation as you felt then. Or you may not have been the child in question, but merely witnessed it happening and also decided it was unsafe to question authority. So, in a current situation, maybe at work, you won't speak up and ask a question. The old experience is determining that decision, not what is happening in the moment. However, if your original question was met with a positive response, you simply won't have this issue.

Old Events Affect Your Decisions around Relationships

Can you remember when you were thirteen or fourteen and you got up the courage to tell a boy or a girl that you liked him or her? How did they respond? Did you feel rejected or embarrassed? Or did you experience a positive response. If it was negative, you may have decided it is never safe to talk about how you feel to someone you love. Did you think there was something wrong with you? When these challenging emotional events are downloaded into your subconscious, it helps you to avoid similar situations. You've got triggers saying, "Don't express your feelings," or you decide you are unlovable. This can become a block when you try to create successful relationships both in business and in your personal life.

The evidence is starting to confirm that in the grip of strong emotion, we react from the age in which the emotion was first triggered. What if you are triggered by an authority figure in the board room, and you react from the trigger age of five? Or worse still, the colleague you are relying on is triggered. Can you see how stress (fear based) can wreak havoc in workplace relationships?

So, if an event activates a trigger you experienced at fourteen, you are going to respond with the emotional resources of a fourteen-year-old. Many of us have an eight-year-old child running significant portions of our lives. This can create havoc in your decision-making process. You make a different decision from an adult's perspective than you do from a child's perspective. So, consider how old events affect your relationships.

Our subconscious fears operate under our conscious radar 24/7. They create resistance and prevent us from deciding what we want to happen. They actually set the energy to attract the very thing we are afraid of. The universal law of resistance is activated: that which we resist persists and drains us of all our energy. In other words, the more we try to avoid something or fear something, the more it stays in our life. Have you noticed this in your life? Have you noticed your patterns? Trauma is relative to the perceiver. It may have been as simple as a spider running up your arm and the fright that ensued.

While our fears show up through our beliefs, our beliefs also show up through our fears. Using relationships as mirrors can be helpful. It is important to note that it's not just negative feelings that can throw us off. Have you ever made a decision through the filter of love or of sexual attraction? Have you let a strong sexual chemistry cloud your decision about a potential partner? We create our sexual feelings through thought, just as we create any other feelings through thought.

It is common to think that the other party makes us feel a certain way. But it is our thought about what is happening that makes us feel. This is the single most important key to an effective decision-making process.

Emotional Attachments Affect Decisions

Just as we have programmed beliefs, we have programmed fears. A lot of those fears were designed to keep us safe. They were helpful when we were kids, but now they are no longer relevant. Some are unspoken, and others are obvious. You probably had many obvious fears in your teenage years, such as in a struggle to be the same as everyone else and still be yourself. How does that happen?

Your thoughts are linked directly to your emotions, and you pick that up by tuning into your body. You can have attachments to doing and being a certain way through your beliefs, and the same is true of your emotions. You can be emotionally attached to situations and to people.

How do you know you are emotionally attached?

1. When you identify with something as being *you*. A good example of this is when you have done a job, and when another criticizes it, you take it personally.
2. When you are too afraid to take action or too afraid not to take action.
3. When you love too much.
4. When there is no logical reason to keep doing something or seeing someone, but you do it anyway.
5. When you feel responsible or take responsibility for another who is capable of looking after him or herself.
6. When you make decisions based on emotions only and don't take logic or gut instinct into consideration.
7. When you find it difficult to let go. E.g relationship, thing, food etc

Being emotionally attached almost feels like an addiction. The corresponding thoughts are usually hidden in old programming. They create the emotions in your subconscious. You won't believe it consciously. Have you ever heard yourself say, "Oh yes, my mother used to say that or do things a certain way, but I don't believe in that myself." But have you checked lately for evidence of your parents' or caregivers' beliefs and emotions showing up in your life?

Emotions Make It Difficult to Make Clear Decisions

A lot of extra time and energy is expended when you need to get something done while dealing with people operating from stress, fear, or another negative emotion. This can significantly affect your decisions and actions throughout our life, relationships, work, etc. Emotions can change your physiology and mask your ability to think clearly. The most frightening thing is that most of us are not aware of this. We have developed sophisticated ways of playing out old tantrums to get our own way or to avoid situations or relationships. This worked very well for us as kids, but it loses its charm and efficiency as we get older.

It is natural for your stress levels to escalate dramatically when you are *subconsciously* driving big projects or relationships from the perspective of a seven- or eight-year-old. Get the picture? We are seeing more ads than ever that represent kids in the boardroom. These behaviors are funny as an advertisement but frustrating in reality.

Others' Emotions Can Affect Your Decisions

Have you ever noticed how your emotions appear to change to match or react to the emotions of the person you are with? It can be difficult to know the difference. When you spend time with negative people, do they bring you down also? This is because the emotions are energy in motion, and they actually resonate at particular frequencies. You may even pick up that a person is angry or sad before they open their mouth to speak.

Or you may notice when you get together with a friend that you feel fine at first, but by the time he has relayed his problem, you feel depressed or angry—even though he seems to be in good humor. By the time he leaves, you are exhausted, and he feels great. Watch out for these "friends." Some friendships are a one-way track—their way!

Do you have a tendency to take responsibility for others' feelings? For example, when you put down the phone after speaking with a distressed friend, you know she feels great because she only wanted you to listen. But you spend the rest of the evening wondering, worrying, or even angry about her problem. So you call the next day and offer help. But she doesn't even remember what she talked about the night before.

Another way this shows up is when you are listening to a friend or colleague and what he says just doesn't feel right. This may be most obvious when you encounter a sleazy salesperson. That never feels good. You know when you've been duped. Often it is more subtle, and you know something is up but may not be able to put your finger on it. These are all signals that can help you adjust your decisions to suit you better. It's about paying attention. Learning how to interpret your signals becomes a huge asset when making decisions in relationships.

When you are in a healthy relationship or friendship, it is easygoing by comparison. You know the old sayings: birds of a feather flock together, we are on the same page, and we are on the same wavelength. Friendships and other relationships are easier when we are on the same or similar energy level.

You probably find it difficult to stay on center with people who operate at different wavelengths from you. For example, people who are ill have low energy levels. You may find it draining to be with them for long. Yet your higher energy will help them feel better. It is important to look after yourself really well when you are caring for sick people.

Others' emotions and emotional well-being can affect your decision-making process. If, for example, your boss is angry about something, and it has nothing to do with you, do you find yourself making decisions and taking action according to his anger? While this is usually a wise course of action, what if you really have to tell her something and you know it will make her madder? Others' moods and emotions affect yours, and it takes strong boundaries to stay on course with your decisions and actions as a result. Here's another example: You are madly in love with your partner. Do you make decisions from love or from clarity?

Why do emotions affect us like this?

New scientific evidence shows us how our limiting beliefs and trapped emotional traumas can mask what is going on in the moment and lead us to play out our past reactions over and over without realizing what we are doing. Equally restricting is consistent or persistent worrying about what is going to happen next. It can hold us in a pattern of fear, making us incapable of responding to what is here now. This limits our potential and our decision-making capacity in every aspect of our life.

- You may have gathered by now that your thought processes alone can throw you a curve ball when making decisions in many ways. You may have wondered why this is so. It creates a feeling in the body, which flows with (experienced as ease) or resists (experienced as resistance) the thought.

This shows up as an emotion. In this case, a lack of awareness of how the body works leads to the belief that your feelings and emotions are a result of what has happened in the outside world. So the feelings feed the thought, which feed the feelings, which feed the thought—and so the cycle continues, escalating the emotions out of proportion with the event.

- Remember that 90 to 93 percent of your thoughts are subconscious, under the radar. Some call the subconscious body wisdom or emotional intelligence. Emotions are governed by the subconscious mind.

- Science is learning more about the effects of fear, stress, and strong emotions. Strong emotions interfere with the rational part of the brain. When you are in the grip of strong emotions like fear, anger, or nervousness, the prefrontal cortex in your brain shuts down. You don't have access to all the intelligence, resources, and capabilities you should have. (See www.pubmed.gov for new discoveries and theories.)

Here are some ways you can tell that your prefrontal cortex is compromised:

- You make a decision when angry that's different to what you'd decide when calm.
- You regret what you say when angry.
- Anxiety leads you to say something silly.
- You're unable to find words to express yourself due to anxiety or other emotion.
- You think of the right answer or more appropriate response when the heat of the emotion has passed.

We all know when we are out of sorts—that is, when we are conflicted within. It presents as confusion, foggy thinking, low energy, indecision, and inability to act, constant doubt, a dragging feeling. These all present the same picture. We are logically swayed toward deciding a particular way, but our gut instinct says different, and our emotions don't know what to do. As much as we know what it is like to be confused or conflicted, we also know how good it feels to be sure about what we want and to take steps to go for it.

How Do You Deal with Your Emotions?

Have you noticed what happens when you get upset about something? Maybe you feel threatened; your reaction happens so fast it is out of your control. What is your first response? Do you verbally disagree? Or is a feeling your first indicator? Or both? Do you notice how the feeling intensifies? Do you notice if you forget the thought that first upset you, it doesn't matter because there are more to back it up? Notice the feelings again. Did you know this happens whether you are actually in an argument with someone or just thinking about it? The brain doesn't know the difference, nor do your feelings, nor do your cells.

The inner biochemical cascade happens in milliseconds. Before you know it, you have generated quite a charge (emotional energy) around the issue. It can play havoc with your decision-making process as both thoughts and feelings work to confuse you.

What are the results? How does this show up in your behavior? You may recognize some or all of the following: defensiveness, taking it personally, being controlling, feeling insecure, needing acknowledgment, being demanding, being unable to share or unable to work in a team, feeling intimidated, undermining, avoidant, needing to be spoon-fed, sulking, being aggressive, causing conflicts, believing everybody else is wrong, feeling isolated or isolating yourself. These are but a few. Do any sound familiar?

There is nothing like a calm, balanced space from which to make a decision; it is very difficult to make a decision that works for you from a space of fear and stress. So how do you deal with your emotions? It's not easy, but it's likely easier to resolve emotions than you think. Research shows that you can dissipate emotions in approximately ninety seconds.

Now that you know that the thought creates the emotion that you feel as a sensation in your body, you can start to work your emotions differently when making decisions. Here are a few examples of how you can do that:

- Pay attention to your thought. Nine times out of ten, if you feel tension in your body, the thought will be fearful or judgmental (of you, of other, or of what is happening).
- Question the truth of your thought. Try to find a more pleasant thought about the subject, or disengage the thought by tuning into your body. (The more you engage the thought, the more intense the emotion and physical tension.) The thought may well be true, but knowing how the emotion thwarts the decision-making process, disengaging from the thought is like stepping back and taking in the bigger picture.
- Tune in to your body. When you notice what's happening in your body, in response to your thought, and recognize the emotion (positive

or negative), it becomes possible to make a decision based on the information available. The decision will be based on emotional information rather than on your reaction to an emotion. For example, I don't feel good about this, so I choose not to act until I have more information. Or, I feel really good about this, so I choose to decide and act on the information I have.

- Breathe deeply, focusing on your heart area. Touching your heart area might help too. Breathe in through your nose and out through your mouth while visualizing the breath as if you are breathing through your heart. Breathe this way for a minute or two until the emotional intensity diminishes. It is recommended that we breathe six cycles in a minute.
- This is reflected in your body as calm or ease.
- You are now in a position to make a clear decision.

The idea is to determine if the emotion was triggered by a past incident or related to the issue at hand. For example, you may feel intense fear when standing up to address an audience. Would you believe that fear of public speaking beats fear of death to the number-one fear spot in the United States? Your fear is likely to be triggered by a memory, and you would feel the same response if confronted with a real danger. You may also feel intense fear when trying something different or new. This tells you that you are stepping out of your comfort zone. It is usually an indicator that you are right on track when explored with the rest of the information available. Once you have ruled out bears and mortal threats as triggers for the fear that is.

I don't have to tell you how emotional energy builds up in your body. Anyone who feels stress can describe the buildup of tension as the workday progresses. Stress is a symptom of fear. Just like we discard excess fluids through our kidneys, we also need to dissipate the charge of pent-up emotions from our body. (Some of the exercises above will help, and I will describe more in chapter 8.)

This is why physical exercise and healthy breathing is so important. Bringing the emotional cascade back into balance is an important way of maintaining balance in the body. I see this with my dog. Her system goes into full alarm when she sees the postman. The hair goes up on the back of her neck, she barks, and immediately afterward she shakes the whole thing off. Unfortunately, we humans don't shake it off that easily.

So, what about the role of the body in decision making?

Chapter Eight

Noticing Physical Sensations

How Do the Body Senses Affect the Decision-Making Process?

The body is the vehicle we use to carry out the action that is a result of the decision. Thoughts, emotions, and body senses are all connected. I describe them separately only because we are used to separating them. Your body is an amazing supersensory being that reflects your thoughts and emotions through body senses. It is responding to what you think about your world at every moment. How do you know? You feel it!

There is so much movement and change happening in our body at any given moment, it seems odd how difficult we find change. As energy moves through your body (emotion), the flow is maintained and you feel at ease. However when the energy flow is resisted (such as when you are in fear, trying to avoid something, feeling conflicted or unsure), it gets stuck, and you feel it as discomfort, tension, or pain. The body senses influence the action according to your decision. *The bottom line is that your thought remains an idea until you take action. The thought directs the action, and the emotion fuels it.*

Simply put, your body responds to a thought regardless of whether it is conscious or unconscious. It doesn't judge, and it does what it is told. So your limiting beliefs show up as actions and behaviors that support those beliefs—for example, habits, learned behaviors, and routines. In fear, your body may go into a freeze response in which you feel like it is dangerous to proceed. But in reality, it may be an old fear showing up, and your inaction may result in a missed opportunity.

How Physical Senses Influence Your Decisions

Maintaining the status quo. Your habitual ways of doing things become a comfort zone. You know what is coming next. You live the way you learned to, and when you do things your way, you know what the result is going to be. It's comfortable, and it's what you are used to. You may or may not like the outcome, but it is better than facing the discomfort of trying something new. Your decision usually supports your comfort zone.

Change. Change always challenges our comfort zone, so our decisions usually keep us in "the zone." We often interpret our conflicted feelings as "this doesn't feel right" or "there is something funny (peculiar) about this," and often we won't take the action as a result. Then the excuses kick in as to why this doesn't need to happen right now. Really, we are pros at this.

See how you stay in a rut? Every time we try something new, we experience conflict, fear, or discomfort. Yet once the new task becomes familiar, we enter our comfort zone again—a *new* comfort zone. So a conflict or discomfort is not always a sign of something bad; it is often an indicator of an old limiting belief that is trying to protect you from trying something new. But the result is often the same, as the decision may be not to take action. Take physical training for example; the first week or two of a new exercise program can be 'painful' as the body gets used to the new activity. For some, this discomfort is enough to stop them pursuing the exercise. For others they know once the first week or two is over they will feel a lot better.

Betrayal. You may get the feeling that your body is betraying you at times. For example, you know the foods that will nourish you and those that don't. But you still end up doing what doesn't work for you. You date that guy that treats you badly, eat that food that doesn't nourish you, take that one drink too many, stay in that dead-end job, leave that positive, nourishing relationship because it scares you. Why is that?

Your head says no—and by the "power of the unknown" you do it anyway. You sabotage or hijack potential success. This is usually an unconscious pattern represented by a craving; your head says, "Stop doing these things," and your body says, "No way, I'm doing this", "I need this" or "But it makes me feel better". Sound familiar? This is your unconscious mind telling your brain, "You need this to protect you." It's not true, but it has more emotional charge than your logic, so it wins out every time.

Pain. Pain in the body is a reflection of resistance to flow. It also presents as the gateway to dissolve that resistance. What do I mean by that?

Very few people are happy about pain. In general, it is the signal to stop what you are doing and pay attention. I have learned that pain has many interpretations. Sometimes we use pain to seek attention—"They will stop visiting if I get better"—or to avoid taking that next step—"I was sick the day of the interview, so I didn't get the promotion." When you exercise and feel pain, do you stop or do you exercise through it? Or do you do both? We can choose to act on messages as time moves on, or we can ignore them.

Maybe you pop a painkiller or apply a makeshift remedy. Or you decide to eat foods that contribute to the pain rather than ease it. The longer you ignore the messages, the more likely pain will start to appear more consistently, and it will be only a matter of time before you are presenting yourself to your doctor or healer with a full-blown illness, needing medication or a treatment of some kind. Pain definitely influences our decisions. It is designed to.

Why do we Misread Our Body Signals?

When we are young, we are told to do or not to do different things. While these instructions may have worked for our caregivers, we may feel discomfort when doing it. Because our carers make it okay, we learn to override our discomfort to fit in or to do what we were told. The more we do this, the more we override our body wisdom and pay more attention to how things "should" be done. Over time we lose trust in our gut instincts and learn to misinterpret how they work for us. I have a theory about some of the times small kids ask why. A parent's request creates a conflict (body resistance) within them that they don't understand, so they ask why. The parent gives a reason, and if the kid agrees with it, that's it; override complete. The child decides to add parental meaning to her feeling and the association is made and locked into the unconscious memory bank. Every time she feels that sensation in her body, she attaches the old meaning and makes decisions accordingly.

Another way we do this is to interrupt an emotion cycle before it is complete. It may be because we were unable or not allowed to express ourselves or experience ourselves in the moment. It may be as simple as being told not to be afraid or to stop crying. You may try not to cry, try not to show anger, or try not to show you are hurt.

In that moment, the energy flow stops; it was interrupted before it had a chance to complete its natural cycle. A decision is made: "It is not safe to do that." The subconscious stores the lack of completion and creates a "bypass" story that protects us from experiencing or doing that thing again. This is usually fear driven and is experienced as tension in the body. The pattern is locked in. Trouble is, even though you may forget about it five minutes later, the memory is still locked in to your unconscious mind for future reference.

Getting to Know Your Senses

The body has one main function: to work incessantly to achieve balance, regardless of our thought processes—conscious or subconscious. It doesn't have a need to judge an incident as right or wrong. It strives for balance and flow, simply. Over time, the body seeks to complete these old mismatches to restore peace and harmony. How does this manifest itself? *We subconsciously seek the experiences that created the old patterns so that our body has opportunities to complete the cycle and restore balance.* This turns up internally through illness, a recurrent injury, or an accident, or externally through life experience, such as feeling stuck, making a career change, or having a relationship conflict.

Your body is transmitting subtle messages all the time. The most common ones are those that indicate hunger or thirst or a need to use the bathroom. You don't have to think about these. You feel it and then take the action your body is requesting. You don't argue with it. You don't need to. It is what it is. Most of us work fine with it. These senses are designed so that we can meet our basic needs. Our mismatches are familiar also; you may find you say things like "Such-and-such event happened years ago, and I have been affected this way ever since."

Emotions show up initially as subtle physical senses also, and they communicate to us all the time. But we haven't learnt to interpret them as we have hunger for example. We have learned to respond other ways. We have learned to judge negative emotions and to try to avoid them to maintain a status quo. This is what creates discomfort in the body. The more you resist or try not to feel, the stronger the sense gets in your body. We call this stress. Think about it, if you ignore your body signals to indicate hunger, what happens? The signals escalate. Well it is the same with emotions.

The body presents emotion in different ways based on how you learned or experienced them. For example, you may feel sadness in your chest; fear in your stomach; anger in your head and shoulders; and depression as general physical weariness. You may feel passion in your stomach; joy in your heart; and happiness all over.

If you struggle with public speaking, you will probably feel fear in a number of ways: a dry mouth, heaviness in your chest, difficulty breathing, blood rushing to your head, a sick feeling in your stomach, or a strong feeling of wanting to run away. These feelings all find expression in our day-to-day language.

We have many sayings and nuances where our body parts are included in our conversations (I am not talking about body language here, which is an art of itself). They are so commonplace that we hardly notice ourselves speaking them and take even less notice of what they might mean. Here are some examples:

- I am out of my *mind*.
- I'm not sure how to *handle* this.
- I can't *stomach* what's happening.
- It *galls* me.
- I had to *back* out of that deal.
- I can't *see* that working.
- He is being a pain in the *neck*.
- I can feel it in my *bones*.

How do I know the difference between what's real and what's an old pattern? All feelings are real, but when you question the truth of the situation, you can establish the realness as true or false. Consider, for example, "I feel really terrified of that spider." Is that really true? The spider is not poisonous. "I learned to be terrified of spiders" is the truth.

How Do I Develop Body Sense?

Body sense is otherwise known as gut instinct. When it is clear, you know you can't ignore it, regardless of the logical indicators. It is different from fear/anger or emotion. It is a clear *knowing*, and when you make decisions based on it, it is difficult to go wrong.

The flow of energy (emotion) is constantly informing you. The subtle messages of flow and resistance constantly tell you to rebalance or adjust a decision or a direction you are considering. It's like retuning a radio to maintain the best sound, retuning a guitar, or changing your route when you come to a detour. When you ignore the messages, stress is born and all that comes with it. When you learn to interpret your mind-body-emotion link as described in the previous chapter, it becomes easier to take action or to intercept, because you now know the action takes you back to center, which is felt as ease in your body. You are now making your decisions using your gut instinct instead of emotional reaction.

Restoring Balance in Your Body

1. *Movement.* Stretching or exercise of any type not only helps restore physical ease but also alters your emotional charge.
2. *Learn your body's yes answer.* Take a few deep breaths and create calm in your system. Now say yes to yourself a number of times. Pay attention to your body senses. You will feel an open

sensation, often in the chest area. A full-body openness is a strong yes. My clients describe this in a number of ways, such as a light feeling in the body, a mind clear of negative thoughts, and no or neutral emotions. Some describe it as a tingling sensation.

3. *Learn your body's no answer.* Take a few deep breaths and create calm in your system. Now say no to yourself a number of times. Pay attention to your body senses. You will notice a slight restriction or heaviness. Again, this is different from fear and is a gut instinct response.

4. *Learn your bodies 'maybe' answer.* Take a few deep breaths and create calm in your system. Now say maybe to yourself a number of times. Pay attention to your body senses. You will notice a sensation different to the other two. Know these responses are unique to you.

5. If you feel pain, *seek the appropriate medical attention.* This information is not intended to replace medical advice or treatment in any way.

6. *Get a massage,* chiropractic treatment, or energy treatment.

7. *Try other alternative sources.*

Our bodies can put us on the right track decision-wise, as our senses reflect what our thoughts and feelings are doing. Imbalance shows up as tension, pain, or illness at extreme levels. I have often *thought* a certain course of action would be ideal for me, tuned into my body answer, and found it to be no. When I override that response, I often regret it. You may see pain as the body saying stop, and it is. Pain is also a valuable tool that helps us unhook old patterns. The main emotion under any pain is fear and or anger. Balance shows up as flow and ease.

Chapter Nine

The Great Unknown (or So We Thought)

*L*ife is a battle for some and a game for others. It has become much easier for me since I became acquainted with the spiritual laws. Spiritual laws teach you how to see your world as a mirror (everything in your world: people, things, events) It is good to remember this when you are trying to change something or someone. As that person is reflecting you, any attempt to change him or her is futile. This represents the law of reflection.

Be the change you want to see in the world.
Mahatma Gandhi

You may have figured this out already: you can only fix yourself. If you look in the mirror and you look tired and drawn, you don't try to change the mirror; you address your diet and get some good sleep.

You likely have heard of the following spiritual laws:

- *The law of karma:* you reap what you sow, and as you give, so you receive.
- *The law of attraction:* You are like a magnet, unconsciously transmitting energy. You attract like energies and repel others. Have you ever felt on the same wavelength as someone? The relationship feels easygoing. You draw toward you everything and everyone who is in your life, whether you like it or not.
- *The law of projection:* You do not know how anyone feels or is. Everything you see in another is a projection of an aspect of yourself. This can work two ways. You may say, "You're weird," to a friend, in which case you are projecting (unconsciously) an aspect of your weirdness onto him or her. It is more comfortable to imagine that someone else has the qualities we wish to deny are within ourselves. The converse is also true. You may see greatness in others, not realizing it is a reflection of greatness in you. My

mentor advised me to emulate and not idolize my teachers.

- *The law of attachment:* You can have anything you wish, but if your sense of self-worth or your happiness depends on having it, you are attached to it.

So, how do the spiritual laws affect the decision-making process? Knowing how these laws work will affect yours dramatically.

1. It helps you easily identify what you can control and know to make your decision as a result.
2. It helps you easily identify what you can't control and to realize that, unless you are deciding for a kid or dependent elderly relative, you can decide only for yourself. You can't make decisions for others.
3. It helps you identify old beliefs lurking in your subconscious, hijacking your attempts to move forward. For example, a belief that you are not good enough may lead you to decide that a dream is out of your reach. Your decision will be made based on your belief and not on what you want to achieve. You won't take the actions that bring that dream into reality.

The purpose of spiritual laws, like all the other laws, is to maintain a balance. Imbalance can start when you don't know how the spiritual laws work. It might feel like you are a victim of your own life, like life is happening to you and you have absolutely no control over your decisions or actions. You make decisions based on what you have learned, and you may find that your decisions are made in reaction to what is happening rather than in response. Blame and judgments are difficult to avoid.

For example, Joan was unaware of the effects her negative attitude had. She felt life was against her, and she spent most of her days complaining about colleagues to whoever was willing to listen to her. She started receiving coaching because there was no one left who would listen—so she had to pay to continue venting her negativity. In the first session, I told her about the spiritual laws and how her external conflicts were a reflection of the conflicts within. Needless to say, Joan was not happy. In her mind, she was paying me to collaborate with her complaining. But she learned that her negative approach to life was attracting the very things she complained the most about. It wasn't long before she changed her tune.

Being unaware of the laws can affect your life.

- When you are unaware of the law of karma (cause and effect), you may not understand that your decisions and actions create a certain outcome. Every decision acted on has an effect. Every decision not to act also has an effect.

- When you are unaware of the law of attraction, you may not realize that your thoughts and feelings generate an energy that attracts similar energy to you. The energy we create unconsciously also has an effect, and it is important to remember that we rarely deliberately invite or attract negative experiences.

- If you are unaware of the law of projection, you may find that you decide to leave a job because you don't like your angry boss. When you understand the laws and work with them, you may be surprised to realize that you may be uncomfortable expressing your own anger. Or you may fear conflict and angry people. Anger is one of the most difficult emotions for humans to deal with. And according to the law of attraction, when you address your anger and learn to channel it into an action that works for you, you attract much calmer people. You may still leave your job, but it will be because you choose to rather than in reaction to your boss's temperament.

- As for the law of attachment, a colleague of mine needed to sell her house because it made sense to downsize. Her attachment to the house and the memories created in it interfered with her ability to make the decision to sell.

Consider the Spiritual Laws When Making Decisions?

These universal laws work whether we like it or not, whether we believe them or not. Remember, beliefs are true only as long as we agree with them. In the same way, nature has four seasons, so working with them, rather than against them, will always work in your favor.

For example, there is no point in driving on the wrong side of the road; you might get yourself killed. It works best for everybody when we follow the rules of the road. Working the spiritual laws brings you into the driver's seat of your life and allows you to reclaim your power from the situations and relationships that don't work for you. You know—the relationships you stay in way longer than you needed to or the job from hell that you can't quite convince yourself to leave. Or maybe you're eating the foods that support weight gain, not weight loss. The spiritual laws are good to know when making decisions, because they help you discern when and in what situations to go with the flow and when not.

Using Spiritual Laws to Call Out Unconscious Beliefs

The best way to use the spiritual laws is to look at your life and what is happening that you want to change. The things that you are least happy with are keys into your subconscious that help you to unlock hidden commitments and beliefs. The law of attraction, for example, may cause you to attract angry people if you are uncomfortable with anger. Or you may attract controllers if you fear taking control. Basically your life is an exact reflection of your beliefs and feelings, whether you are aware of it or not. While this may be frustrating to accept, it becomes a golden nugget in decision making when you can work it in your favor instead of being a victim of it.

A key here is that you don't change your outside world until you change its match within. You can run from a relationship, keep changing jobs because of crazy bosses, avoid uncomfortable emotions, but the next relationship is the same: the boss is crazier, the emotions don't go away.

You can't run away from yourself.

The very fact that we have learned to blame work for being stressed or the boyfriend/girlfriend for the relationship not working the way we want shows that we deprive ourselves of the ability to decide for ourselves in a given situation. We remain victims. The truth is, we become stressed in work some days more than others. We have less tolerance when tired than we do after a good night's sleep.

If we work the spiritual laws, however, we can read a situation or event differently, and by asking a number of simple questions, we can reclaim our right to decide whether or not the situation works for us. We then choose whether or not to continue taking part and/or to redefine a boundary that leads to a healthy outcome for us. The decision-making process becomes a lot easier.

So the spiritual laws offer us the wisdom to take full responsibility for our thoughts, emotions, and actions. If you do not understand spiritual laws, you may be inclined to blame and complain about what is happening outside you. This is what we learned to do, and it keeps us embroiled in drama. For example, a friend is upset about her latest crisis. Do you get carried away by her drama and become upset with her? Or do you listen and support her? I equate this to rescuing someone who is drowning. Do you jump in and risk drowning yourself? Or do you throw a life buoy and let her help herself. Of course you can jump in with the life buoy to help her without compromising your own safety. If we jump into every crisis and react emotionally, who's in control? I believe our success is determined by how calm we can stay in a crisis, not by the level of stress we can create.

If you are ready to learn what you need to do to shift your perspective and your life, you are in the right place. The spiritual laws are the easiest way to uncover subconscious beliefs or agreements. And when you change what you think, you change your perspective. Your decisions and subsequent actions change, and the outcome becomes what you want—or something better.

Working with the spiritual laws can be tricky at first, but the results speak for themselves. As long as blaming or denial is in play, so is drama. This means you are focused on what is happening outside you as the cause for your concern. You may have noticed that you can't control this. What you can control is what you are thinking about the event, and that is your inner game. In other words, the sooner you can quit shifting the blame and open up to what you may be learning, the sooner you can shift your reality.

The spiritual laws are at the heart of every religion and spiritual tradition. Aligning your lives with these laws transforms relationships, health, wealth, love, and self-expression. There are some simple questions to ask while aligning with the spiritual laws to enhance your decision-making process.

- What is happening exactly?
- What am I learning from this situation, relationship, etc.?
- Why would I need this in my life?
- Is it/he/she working for me?
- What do I want instead?

Every relationship and life situation is a teacher. While it is not always easy to look for a lesson, life and relationships get much easier when you do. Let's see how you can use the spiritual laws to identify unconscious patterns or beliefs that are causing you to make decisions that may not serve you.

Law of Karma

Have you noticed that behaving in certain ways often dictates the outcome of a situation? If you are pleasant, your friends are pleasant back. The converse is also true. If you are grumpy, you will get a different response. So, what is happening in your life that doesn't work for you?

Ask yourself, How am I contributing to this outcome? Or how am I keeping this scenario in place? When you ask this, you bring your attention back to you. It makes sense to do this, as you can affect *only* your own environment. Can you identify a behavior pattern? Is there a belief underlying the behavior? Do you find yourself saying, "I always do this because ..." or "This is who I am" or "This is the way I have always done things. I'm just quirky"? Really, you are behaving in a way to comply with that belief or pattern.

When you ask the questions above, you get to be honest with yourself. Ask yourself if this particular situation is really working for you. What excuses are you using to keep it in your life? Are those excuses really true?

Now you are ready to decide. What do you want to achieve? How can you live differently to create the outcome you want? What actions can you take? Sometimes you may need to look for another job, for example, or leave a relationship. You will find that once you make the decision to take a different action or to behave differently, you will get a different outcome and response.

Law of Attraction

You attract people, events, and happenings every second of every day, whether you like it or not. As I mentioned previously, your unconscious is working away under the radar 24/7, so there is a lot going on in your being that your are unaware of.

Ask yourself this question: What is happening exactly? And I mean *exactly*! Are you ill again? Have you attracted another jerk—different face, same pattern? Have you backed out on your healthy plan again? Are your friends showing up for you, and are you showing up for them?

One of my clients was applying for a job recently. She had great credentials and experience, and the interview process went on for much longer than usual; the company kept calling her back for interviews. It was as if they couldn't make up their minds. I asked if her mind was made up about the job. She realized she wanted a job and hadn't quite made up her mind that this was it. The company was mirroring her indecision back to her.

She explored what was happening in the interview process and checked to see where she had not made up her mind. She refocused on her purpose for applying for that job in the first place. And she decided to commit fully to the process. She was offered the job in the next interview.

Have you ever noticed this in your life? Can you tell when someone isn't engaged in a conversation? Sometimes it's obvious; at other times the person is saying all the right things but something just doesn't feel right. It is hard to put a finger on it. You say you want to do something, but because you don't decide on what action to take, nothing happens. Or, like my client, you go through the motions of the interview and indecision shows through your energy and is reflected back accordingly.

Use the law of attraction to explore what underlying beliefs or thoughts that attract what you do not want. These beliefs are often things you heard growing up and that you no longer believe now, but the results are telling you that they are running under the radar. Remember, the belief with the highest "charge" gets the result.

Law of Projection

You think everyone thinks and feels the same way you do. And you see your faults and star qualities in others. This is where blame and judgment hang out and can be called out. Every time you assume to know what another feels or is, you are projecting. It is difficult to accept this law, as so much of our perceptions and what we have learned are projections.

Most of us don't realize how much we do this. It is a powerful form of denial.

Projecting your stuff onto someone else prevents you from taking responsibility for yourself. Our hidden or unconscious beliefs show up in our judgments and projections. The saying "a pot calling the kettle black" describes the law of projection well. Neither sees itself as black. Instead, each sees how black the other is. Everything you see in another is a projection of an aspect of yourself.

The question to ask here is, "What do I see in (person's name) that I don't see in myself?" Or "Where do I need to take responsibility for myself?" Or "Where am I making a decision based on what she is doing/saying? Where am I making someone wrong?"

Good examples of projections are generalizations like "the world is a dangerous place," "everybody does it this way," "I feel you are being nosy," "it is difficult being a business owner," "she is amazing," "he is so kind," "she must be feeling terrible."

In reality we experience life from our unique perspectives. When we take full responsibility for ourselves, we may say instead, "I feel threatened by what is happening in the world," "I do things this way," "That is my business," "I find it difficult being a business owner," "I am amazing," "I am so kind," "I feel terrible?" This process is empowering because we allow our experience and allow others to have theirs.

I had a colleague who "believed" we should all believe the same way she did and was easily offended if that was not the case. Not only did she not allow us to have our own opinion, but she also saw us in complete disagreement if our opinion differed. Not understanding this law has led people into all sorts of trouble.

Use the law of projection to explore decisions you make in response to others. Are you making decisions based on what they say? Or based on what you learned? Or because you are afraid you will hurt their feelings? Or are you making decisions based on what you want? In some traditions, making decisions based on what you want is considered selfish, but this is not true. It is possible to make decisions with respect to others (win/ win) and not despite them or you.

The Law of Attachment

We can be attached to ways of doing things, ways of thinking, and ways of behaving. Nobody likes change right? Well, when our attachments prevent us from making decisions that allow us to move our lives forward, we become stuck. Get the picture?

It starts young. A child won't go to sleep without her teddy or security blanket. As we grow older, being attached to doing things a certain way, even though we don't like the outcome, becomes a trap. The questions to ask here are "Do I really need to do it this way?" "Do I really need this in my life?" "Do I really need this person?" "Do I really need to live in this house to be happy?"

I had a client recently who strongly felt she needed to be stressed to the hilt before she would do anything; she didn't see another way of working. Surprisingly, a lot of people believe that stress is their main motivator. We wear stress as a badge of how hard we work while we complain about it all the while. Are we more attached to stress or to the complaining? Who knows? After a couple of weeks of coaching, the client started to ask, "Do I really need to stress about that? Is there another way to go about it?"

This is a good method for uncovering old beliefs underneath "I have to do this or else" and "If I don't do it this way, I will get in trouble." What response would you get if you changed up a tradition? We had steak for Christmas dinner one year; it was the favorite dinner for my partner and kids. When I told my family at home, they thought we were weird. It was just dinner! What response do you get when you want to try something new?

Use the law of attachment to uncover underlying beliefs that keep you doing things a certain way. What decisions are you making as a result?

I work with my clients to help them consciously attract what they want by identifying the old beliefs and shifting the energy around them. They are then in a position to make clear, clean decisions and to commit to the direction they chose. Life works best when the old constraints are removed like this. If not, the new ideas become stifled among the old patterns. It would be like just removing the leaves of a weed and leaving the root in the ground.

It is important to note that you are here to experience your world. Your feelings and emotions are evidence of how you are responding in any given moment. You are going to be pulled off center; you are going to be distracted. This is all part of life. The key is to realize that those pulls don't define who you are or what you do. Your ability to be present does. So worrying about what was done or about what hasn't happened yet keeps you distracted from where you are at your best, which is in the here and now. When you do find yourself worrying, acknowledge the feeling (in other words, be present to the feeling). Establish what is in your control. Notice what isn't in your control. Then do what you can, and let go of what you can't.

Being present to all your feelings without needing to judge them is key. It is the easiest way to convert the tension back to flow in the body.

There are two days of the year where nothing
can be done; one is called yesterday and the
other is called tomorrow. Today is the right
day to love, believe, do and mostly live.
Dalai Lama

We flow and ebb with life as naturally as we breathe. Realizing this is ultimate wisdom.

We were meant to live in community, and we learn most from relationships. How equal are your relationships? If someone needs you, do you drop everything to help? Or does it depend on the circumstances? Do you find yourself hatching emergencies with everybody else so you can avoid being with yourself? Or do you use looking after yourself to avoid connecting with or helping someone else? Now we are back in tricky territory.

Many of my clients believed that putting others first was the order of things and usually at their expense. There is a good reason for the airlines to recommend putting on your own oxygen mask first. Going for win-win dynamics supports the cooperative model rather than the competitive and controlling model—even if we have the best intentions.

Balance in relationships is what the world is striving for. It is a new way for most, because the battle of cultures and belief systems maintains inequalities.

Even the best systems and practices become skewed when out of balance.

Making your decisions from that balanced perspective contributes to bringing a new aliveness into your relationships.

Last but not least, learn how to read external signs. For centuries, the human race has viewed the outside world as a yardstick to measure against instead of as a mirror to work with. It can get out of hand when we see reality through superstitions or voodoo. If you believe something works, it is true for you, and you will create that in your reality. If you believe a drug works, it probably does. If you believe it doesn't, it won't. Doctors can tell you that many of their patients can override the efficacy of a drug if they don't believe in it. That said, reading the world and your relationships, as a mirror of you can be a lot of fun. Everything mirrors your thoughts, including your emotions, your physical well-being, and your relationships.

Notice what is happening in your life and use that to pinpoint old habits that may influence your decisions so that you take actions to support your current habits, not the change you want.

In summary, what's happening outside you is reality. It's how you think and feel about it that becomes your experience of that reality.

So how do you pull all this together?

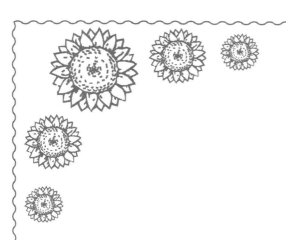

Part 3

Making Decisions
That Work for You

Chapter Ten

Take Back Your Power

*M*ost people want to know that they are making the right decision from the start. Before they go out with someone, change their job, or move, they want to know they are making the right choice. Sometimes this is possible. But more often than not, many factors out of your control determine the outcome.

It is necessary to try many things out and decide what works for you. This often creates fear that can actually keep you from trying new things. Experts, word of mouth, and referrals all have great value and can help you narrow your scope and focus your decision in a particular direction. You can find how to in books or from a mentor, but there always comes a time when you have to make up your own mind. Knowing that most information acts as a guide to inform your process is a big step in awareness. When you understand that only you have your own answers, you take back your power from others and empower the decision process to work for you.

Decision making is a continuous process. You make decisions every day, and they help you to navigate the course you want your day to take. You are probably tuned into your survival needs. Your body gives you signals when you are hungry, thirsty, tired, and so on—and you fulfill your requirements accordingly. But sometimes the signals are not as clear. The five-elements process takes decision making to a new level and can help you navigate both known and unknown territory. It is easier than you think. The decision challenge is to develop clarity, certainty, and confidence that result from all your intelligences aligning.

When you tune into your complete intelligence, you can rule out a number of choices, knowing they are not for you. This can save you a lot of time, money, and effort. You can always check in later to see if the decision is still valid based on the outcomes. It may or may not be, and you reserve the right to change your mind. In fact, it is important to know that decisions aren't forever; you will always be adjusting your course based on your goals as your life unfolds.

Acting on a decision can take courage if that decision is contrary to popular opinion or your family's ideals. However, I encourage you to persist, because the self-confidence and trust you gain from making your own mind up are the secrets to reclaiming and creating the life that you want.

This makes sense. You are here to live your life, not somebody else's.

Before you go any further, review the body yes and no exercise and practice it until you are comfortable with your ability to identify your responses. Remember the five key elements: thoughts, emotions, body senses, unconscious mind, and spiritual laws. Using the information provided on each of the key elements, you can better make the decision that works best for you.

How Does It All Fit Together?

Once you establish goals, your decisions are necessary to determine the direction you will take. A decision comprises the first three elements: thought, emotion, and body sense. The idea is to include all the information available to you externally and internally.

Thinking of what you want generates an emotion, which you feel in the body. When all three are aligned, you feel ease; when they are not, you feel conflicted. Limiting beliefs and their corresponding emotions can mask the process.

The outcome determines the use of the fourth and fifth elements. If you are happy with the outcome, keep going by deciding and taking actions to realize your goals. If you are unhappy with the result, go back to chapter 9 and use the spiritual laws to explore the hidden patterns, beliefs, and fears that are keeping you from

- connecting with what you want,
- making decisions that serve you,
- taking subsequent actions, and
- realizing your goals.

The best indicator for this is your inner compass, your body feelings, as they are an expression of your thoughts and emotions. In general, we do not choose or decide to do something that doesn't work for us unless we firmly believe it is necessary (limiting belief). Below are a number of scenarios with which you may be familiar and the different responses. Use these as guidelines to help you make decisions in the future.

Flags for When You Are about to Make a Big Decision

For a definite yes decision:

- Your mind is clear, you know what you want, and the question is "Does this decision align with my goal?"
- Your emotions are neutral or calm.
- This shows up as ease in your body.
- You decisions are clear, and it is easy to take action.
- You get the outcome as you wanted, and you are satisfied with the results.
- Next decision, next step.

For a yes decision when you think you know what you want, based on what you learned to want:

- Your mind is clear.
- Your emotions are calm.
- You feel at ease in your body.
- The decision is clear, and it is easy to take action.
- The outcome is as you expected but doesn't satisfy you as much as you thought. You feel disappointed or empty as a result of the outcome, rather than happy.

It is possible that you are upholding a family goal that you believe in (but that may not work for you). You are in a comfort zone because the goal is so familiar to you that you don't know any different. What you do know is that you are not happy with the result. This shows in your body as low energy and a feeling of resignation, lethargy, frustration, emptiness, or a lack of fulfillment.

Inherited beliefs mask the decision process. An unhappy feeling as a result of the outcome can mean a couple of things. You may be fulfilling a genuine want, and your belief system doesn't allow you to enjoy it. Or the goal is inherited, not yours, and you need to decide whether or not you want to continue this course of action. Examples of beliefs that support this include, "I am not worthy," "I don't deserve this," "It's too easy; something is going to go wrong."

Emotions can mask the decision process also. An example of this is when you repeat relationship issues over and over. The body is saying no, and you override it by misreading the signal as "chemistry" or love. Say you had an emotionally unavailable parent growing up. There is a very good chance you will attract an emotionally unavailable partner as a result. Your friends know it, and you know it at a level, but you get involved anyway because it is familiar. It is the behavior that you learned to associate with love.

For a definite no decision:

- Your mind is clear. The question is, "Is this decision aligned with my goal?"
- Your emotions are neutral.
- A part of our body feels contracted. (I feel a subtle contraction in my chest, just above my solar plexus. You may feel it elsewhere.)
- The decision is clear, not to take action at this time.
- You look or wait for the next available option.

For a false no decision due to masking emotions:

- Initially your mind is clear. You know what you want, and it is different from what you are used to. For example, you are contemplating leaving a job to set up a new business, or a transition in your relationship.
- Your emotion is unexpected and sometimes irrational fear.

- Your body feels tense due to fear (or another emotion). This is misinterpreted as a no answer.
- Because of the fear, your mental clarity becomes doubt and confusion.
- Your decision is not to take action at this time.
- Outcome is no change and you continue in the familiar world

But this outcome can lead to unfulfilled goals due to the fear, which kept you from acting. Procrastination and being overwhelmed are commonplace with fear.

The fear is linked to that unconscious belief that was set up to keep you safe and, perhaps, loyal to your tribe. Now you are trying something new, and the fear shows up to keep you from betraying your tribe. There is no danger (for which fear is the flag), so the more realistic action is to process the fear as in chapter 7 and decide on the action that will support your goal. Other fears that lead to this decision process are a fear of success and a fear of failure.

For a false no decision due to masking belief:

- Your mind is clear (You don't know anything different).
- Initially your emotions are neutral.
- Your body is in ease (comfort zone).
- Your decision is not to take action at this time or to take the action to support the belief.
- The outcome here is telling. You may feel like you are settling or resigned. It is not what you want but what you believe you want. You may accept the situation blindly without question and think that this trapped feeling is 'normal'.

Consider the saying "cutting off your nose to spite your face." It means doing what you do—despite the outcome and knowing the results don't work for you—to fulfill a belief.

A typical example of this shows up in relationships. We learn how to be in relationship from our parents and family life. You may find yourself relating to men as you saw your mother relate to your father. However, because you have a different relationship with your parents than you have with your partner, you may find this doesn't work for you in real life. The trouble starts when you try to make your parents' way work because you believe this is how it must be. The belief is setting up the decisions that would work best for your parents, and not for you and your partner. It is likely that your partner never measures up to your preset requirements of who he or she should be. This is far more common than you might think.

For a maybe:

- Your mind is unclear, reflecting doubt or confusion.
- Your emotions may vary or be neutral.
- Your body is contracted (this response can be subtle and is usually in a different location than the *no* contraction).
- Your decision is not to take action.
- The next step: explore your options, as you may need more information before you can make the decision.

It is said that the body doesn't lie. It may be truer to say that the body doesn't judge. If an unconscious pattern is running under the radar, your body senses are very real. A question that needs to be asked here is, is the thought creating them true? And is the meaning you have attributed to them true? Those old fears might present in the same way twenty years later and no longer mean what you think. They may have been true at the time and no longer need to rule your life. Play with the questions you ask. For example, if you have set a goal and it is not working out, ask questions like these:

- Is this goal aligned with your authentic self?
- Is this goal aligned with your true purpose?
- Are you learning from the experience in an easy/ fun way?
- If not, how can you bring more fun and ease into the equation?

We don't have to learn the hard way. Doing things differently from how your family did them can incur unconscious or conscious guilt for being disloyal to the tribe. How do you know? Guilt is always followed by punishment. So if you are aligned with your purpose and it isn't working out, check to see if you have any limiting beliefs that keep you loyal to the tribe at the expense of your goals. You may find yourself sabotaging your success.

The common denominator for this is how you feel in your body. For example, stress is a signal of fear and is felt as tension. The reason a number of professions have extensive training programs is so that, under pressure, the critical decisions are made from the learned skill set rather than from a position of stress/fear

When you feel conflicting senses, don't ignore them. Always question what they are saying without judgment. When in doubt, question your thought process and emotions, and believe in your body senses. Use energy-shifting exercises to discern a yes, no, or maybe answer, and use this to support your decision process.

When the outcome is not what you want, look to the spiritual laws to call out unconscious patterns, beliefs, and fears that prevent you from staying focused on what works for you, which is defined by the increased amount of aliveness you feel. What do you want instead? What actions will get the desired result?

Life is about living on purpose. I searched for many years for my purpose and wondered why no one else could give me the answer. I discovered that life purpose is to do what you do on purpose—from walking the dog to working to relationships to travel. Don't do it because you should. I once heard a mentor say, "Do it for you, do it on purpose, do it because you love it. And because of that, everyone around you will benefit."

When you tune into all your intelligence resources, you are able to make decisions that support you. Combine what you have already learned with your feelings and intuition. When you do not know the answer, instead of fearing change, open to the possibilities that lie ahead— the possibilities that bring the most aliveness when you focus on them being realized in your life.

Now you can see how your ability to trust and know your instincts can rule out a lot of the fear involved in making changes.

As you make decisions and act on them, ask yourself three questions: What do I want? Is it working for me? And what next? Like a finely tuned engine, your emotional and intelligence guidance system will constantly feed you information, which you now know helps you adjust and readjust your decisions as you take steps toward your goals.

Practicing this process regularly you will quickly learn how to trust yourself again, connect with your inner compass and make those decisions that align with your goals.

Making Decisions that Work for You.......

Chapter Eleven

Releasing Attachments

Identifying and Releasing Attachments
Turns Your Issues into Assets

The most important part of the coaching experience is identifying and releasing attachments that act as the glue, keeping you stuck. Learning to identify what you can control and refocusing on what you want allows you to base your decisions on what is in your control rather than what is not. Stepping back from the offending drama is the best way to be open to what is happening in the scenario for you. This is based on the principle that you can change only yourself.

So becoming aware of your old patterns and how they currently affect your decision-making process helps the process considerably. Then use the tools in this book to clear your thoughts and calm your emotions so they don't interfere with the decisions necessary to realize your goals any more. The attachment releasing tools I offer in this chapter are carried out with the following steps in mind.

1. **Learn to be realistic** about what is in your control and what is not.

2. **Get to the truth of the situation.** If it is bothering you—that is, triggering fear, anger, or another response—it's yours to explore. Remember, it's not what is happening that is bothering you; it is what you are *thinking* about what is happening. When you discover what that is, you embrace one more piece of your puzzle. Achieving your dreams becomes a journey of personal discovery instead of an inquisition of what you may be doing right or wrong. Each attachment hides an untapped potential resource.

3. **Accept the situation *as it is now*.** The number-one cause of conflict is arguing with reality.

Learn to deal with what is present rather than what you think should be there.

4. **Reestablish or redefine what you want.** What do you want to achieve? Getting clear on what you really want and not what you think you want is an important part of this process. Realizing what is missing helps you to refocus on what you want.

5. **What new decisions do you need to make?** What new steps can you take to achieve your goals?

Again, the attachment loop has these key components: a belief, a thought, senses in the body, an emotion, and a response. All these components can be used to access a loop and interrupt or dissipate a pattern. Awareness is the key here. In my experience, the attachment pattern is not necessarily wrong, just out of balance. For example, I had a client who tended toward obsessive-compulsive behaviors. Instead of obsessing about what was wrong with her business, she gave her behavior another focus and obsessed instead about the steps necessary to promote a life-work balance. As you can imagine, the strategy proved very useful.

In other words, all assets can become liabilities when we are out of balance. Learning to refocus our behaviors into those that work for us is key here. Remember, most of us don't know what is stopping us. This is why coaching is so valuable; it helps us see and identify our blind spots.

Attachment Release

The most important part of the process is developing the ability to step back from the offensive scenario. In my experience and the experience of my clients, the following are indicators of imbalance:

- **Upholding the blame stance—** that is, it's happening to me, or it's their fault; they are wrong. They may well be wrong, but the point is that you find your balance. Establishing what you need and not focusing what they are doing helps you regain your focus.
- **Attempting to fix something that is out of your control.** You find yourself trying to fix another's business or taking responsibility for others feelings, for example.
- **Doubting yourself,** your instincts and your knowing. You believe someone else or some information rather than trusting yourself. Remember there are as many ways of being human as there are people on this planet. You do 'YOU' better than anybody.

These indicate that you are looking outside yourself for answers and distracting yourself from what is really going on in you. Recognize the outer conflict is a reflection of the inner. To rebalance, you need to check into what is happening in your body.

This is the cutting edge of your personal discovery. Up to now the outer conflict has distracted you from your discoveries. The big lesson here is that you *mind your own business.*

The releasing methods are simple and are designed to shift your attachments to subconscious patterns, habits, and holding patterns. You can then use them to work these patterns in your favor rather than against and to shift stuck energy, defensiveness, emotional stuckness, situational stuckness, relationship stuckness, and so on. The resulting decisions support the changes, and the action steps become easier to complete.

The methods help restore flow to your body, mind, and spirit, putting you in a position to make the decisions that best serve you, your relationships (home and work), and your life.

Whether you are running a country, a business, or a home, this process is invaluable.

1. Reconnect. Adjust Your Breath

A profound shift can come from adjusting your breathing. A number of changes occur when you are stuck; often you operate from the stress response, which is disconnected from your gut instinct/intuition.

> ➤ You may hold your breath.
> ➤ You may start to breathe quicker.
> ➤ You may breath only into your chest.

Breathing deeply into your abdomen aiming for six breaths a minute can help restore balance and flow. Correct breathing can help remove 70 percent of the toxins in your body, and focused breathing is used in many traditions to distract or quiet a busy mind. Breath is an important source of life for us. We can survive without food for weeks and without water for days, but we can survive only minutes without a breath. Also, breathing into the abdomen stimulates the parasympathetic nervous system, which promotes balance.

2. Release External Distractions

You do this by cutting fear-based cords of attachment. This is a wonderful, simple visualization to help you clear all fear-based attachments connecting you to a situation or relationship. Remember that your brain doesn't know the difference between real or imagined. It does what it is told. Have you ever heard the expression "It's time to cut the cords and move on"? This is based on the premise that energy follows thought and the knowing that we are all connected.

We form energy cords/connections to everyone we meet, to things—such as houses, cars, and money—and to ways of behaving. Mostly the cords are healthy. However, we can form cords through fear. You will know because these fear cords keep you from doing or not doing for fear of losing someone or something, rather than doing it because the action is what works best for you.

Gemma came to me because she wanted to meet someone. She complained that everyone she met had something wrong with them; they just didn't do things the way she wanted. She was very unhappy and wondered why she couldn't attract someone who loved her. When Gemma explored her relationships, she saw a theme emerging.

Interestingly, when she cut cords of fear that held her from attracting the guy for her, here's what happened. She recalled a memory of when she was seven or eight years old. She had a wonderful relationship with her uncle; she really loved him. He was kind and accepting and didn't constantly tell her what to do.

But her uncle died suddenly, and she was devastated as she experienced grief for the first time. She didn't know what all the feelings were and didn't know what to do with them. The strongest feeling she described was of betrayal. How could he leave her? Why did he have to die like that?

The most important thing Gemma remembered was that she vowed never to allow herself to feel that way about anyone ever again. She had equated love with betrayal and sadness. Can you see where this is going? The pattern in her relationships was that as she and her partners became more intimate, she found more things wrong with each one.

Energy-wise, Gemma was connecting with her partners through the fear cord that had formed because of her vow. No matter how amazing the guy, she could see only through her vow of fear. "If I love someone, he will leave me," To do this, she had to find things wrong so that she could maintain a safe distance. Every guy she met looked like a jerk through this filter; it was only a matter of time before the relationship would break up. This confirmed her vow that if she loved someone, he would leave her.

Cutting the cords of fear had a dramatic effect on Gemma. She met a new partner a short time later and learned to relate to him differently than she had to others. And yes, the result changed also. They are still together and happy.

To cut cords, do this exercise:

1. Take three deep breaths as you visualize the situation in which you are stuck.
2. Imagine the attachments as cords running between you and the person or incident.
3. Notice what you feel in your body. Where do you feel it?
4. Keep breathing deeply.
5. Ask your body to release all cords or entanglements that keep you from learning what you need to know to move forward.
6. See the cords dissolving or transmuting. Visualize them disappearing completely.
7. Release the effects of those cords consciously and subconsciously, rebalancing your whole energy to that of your essence.
8. Notice changes in your body. Notice thoughts, ideas, and memories.
9. See the other person cleared also.
   Breathe deeply, visualizing yourself and the situation as clear and free.
10. Remain open to other possibilities.

This exercise can be useful in many areas of your life. It can help you to step back and gain perspective on a situation. It also can help you to step out of a blame game and come back to you and what you want to achieve. You can do this in the board room if things are getting heated and you need to create space, or you can do this in meditation form, inviting help from your source (according to your belief). In other words, it can take seconds or minutes. It is up to you. This exercise is a powerful way to reclaim your power from a situation. There are also many variations of this visualization.

3. Reprogram the Beliefs

You do this by developing beliefs that support growth. When your thought process is stuck, it can hold the emotion, the subsequent decisions, and the outcome stagnant. Realizing that your thought process/belief may be limiting you frees you to release the attachment to the belief and seek a different perspective. The idea is to dismantle the limiting belief and create a new perspective that promotes creativity and growth.

You need to bear in mind that if a subconscious limiting belief is in play, engaging your mind may be futile. This is why I suggest a number of ways to release attachments and create different perspectives: mindset, emotion, physical, and energetic. For example, the event you find unsatisfactory in your life can be used to call out the offending subconscious thought process that is keeping you stuck. Remember, you already have all the excuses in the book as to why to keep this belief in play. Your awareness of and honesty with yourself are key.

You may find it easier to make a shift (a change in perspective) through the other aspects before engaging a mental shift. A mental shift occurs quickest when you can shift to gratitude. For example, I am so grateful that this showed up right now; I wonder what I might be learning? This shifts the energy and feelings in your body and opens up exploration. Once the mental shift occurs, you can unhook the emotions and energy related to the old perspective from your body. Use the following questions in the exploration.

- What do I want to achieve here?
- Where is my focus? Is it on the drama? Or is it on the goal I wish to achieve?
- What is the truth of the situation?
- What is in my control?
- What is not in my control?

Establishing what is in your control or not in your control is a critical part of the process. The sooner you can refocus on what is in your control, the better. This question in itself is powerful: "Is this in my control?" It needs to be asked in conjunction with the "what do I want" question. The control question is critical, because many of us believe that we are responsible for others' thoughts, feelings, and actions. We also believe that others are responsible for *our* thoughts, feelings, and actions.

Have you ever been in a bad mood, ruminating over a grievance, when a good friend comes to the door? You are so glad to see your friend that you forget about your drama; your humor and your energy are lifted immediately? This is what the gratitude strategy can achieve. It is one of the most powerful ways to shift negative energy into a place that can dissolve all ills.

4. Reposition Your Body

Do this by accessing your body wisdom. In the course of my studies, the importance of moving the body became clear to me. The body holds certain positions that relate to a conflict. Moving your body shifts the flow of feeling and energy. For example, through natural enthusiasm you decide you are going to get fit, and through overzealousness you overdo it on the first day. You wake up the next morning stiff and sore, and this ends your fitness binge. However, if you had gently stretched your body in the stiff areas, you could have released the lactic acid buildup and opened your body to flow again.

Shifting your body's position creates flow in it again, which means exercise is important. We can remove 50 percent of the toxins in our body through exercise. Any movement that works for you will do, such as a gentle stretch, walk, or dance.

If you feel tension in part of your body—maybe an ache in your shoulder, a twinge in your knee, a headache—use a combination of breath, movement, and enquiry. Ask that part of your body what is it trying to tell you, and allow the answer to surface. It will be the first thing that comes to mind.

The second thing that may come to mind is a comment like "Don't be ridiculous" or "That is silly" or "Are you crazy?" These are all normal. You may even hear a particular voice that sounds familiar. It might remind you of a parent or a schoolteacher. The reality is that your body is trying to tell you something, and the story your body tells is often completely different from what your reasoning mind thinks. The key here is that when you open to the truth of a situation and the truth of the emotion behind the thought, the tension in your body will likely dissipate.

5. Restore Emotional Intelligence

Do this by interpreting the emotions as your guidance system. The best way to unhook emotions is to feel your feelings through their full cycle. As we learned earlier, emotions are a guidance system—unless we attach meaning to them or a story to explain them. The story escalates the intensity of the emotion, and we can lose the information that tells what is really happening. Our emotions are literally our natural response to the thought we are thinking. They aren't good, bad, or indifferent unless we make them so by adding meaning. Making friends with our emotions is the best present we can give ourselves.

When I say to feel through a full cycle, I mean to notice when you first start to feel an emotion and then to breathe deeply through the experience until your body returns to calm. It is best not to attach words to this process. If you do, you may escalate the emotional energy or try to fix it and smooth it over. Or you may make yourself wrong for feeling that way which also escalates the emotion feeling.

Here are a few questions to ask about your emotions:

- Am I taking full responsibility for my emotions?

- Am I acknowledging that I am creating this, or am I blaming someone or something for making me feel this way?
- Have I broken an agreement with another or myself?
- Am I choosing this situation, or am I doing it because I should?
- Am I taking responsibility for someone else's feelings, thoughts, or actions to protect or defend him or her?
- Do I need to redefine or create a boundary?

You may have heard of tapping. This is acupuncture without the needles for emotions; it is a combination of Chinese acupuncture and modern psychology. This is a wonderful, effective technique that restores the flow of energy in the body. You tap gently on different points as you speak of what is bothering you and the emotion you are feeling. Tapping has been scientifically proven to reduce cortisol levels, rewire the brain, and increase the energy flow. It helps with pain relief, can eliminate emotional problems, assists in post-traumatic stress disorder, and helps reduce symptoms of diseases. (See the reference section for more information.)

Combinations

Combining any or all of the above can be very useful. Trying them out adds value, as we all have our own ways of working things. The important thing is that you realize that you don't have to suffer. You can change any circumstance that pertains to what is in your control. And the freedom you receive by letting go or embracing what you can't control ends the world of drama and opens a new world of exciting creativity.

My clients used to say—without the drama—Won't my life be boring? It was never long before they realized that all the time spent in conflict and dramas, repeating relationships and events that they didn't want, was replaced with their conscious creation of what they wanted. They were excited to do what they loved and to realize their dreams easily. In time they learned to alter their perspective on change and their fear of the unknown to that of embracing the opportunity. Remember fear is excitement without the breath.

Once you begin transforming attachments, you are freed to make decisions based on what you really want, rather than on your programmed wants. So you become mentally clear, committed, and not emotionally attached. You are freed to connect with your creativity instead of running old patterns; you undo them and create what you really want. The decision-making process becomes one of alignment among your thoughts, learned assets, emotions, and feelings. You know you are on track because the yes feels light and easy, and the no feels heavy and tense.

Chapter Twelve

Reasons to Seek Coaching

You can only resolve that created in
relationship through a relationship.
Annita Keane

Blind Spots and the Benefits of the Coaching Process

Contrary to popular belief, coaching is not another form of therapy. It doesn't mean there is something wrong with you. It is a process people engage in when they want to take their life to the next level. They know where they want to be and due to blind spots or glass ceilings (i.e. limiting beliefs) there is a gap between where they are now and where they want to be. The decisions that have created their current results do not support the changes they want to make: getting that promotion, finally breaking out to set up their own business, moving jobs, seeking that new relationship etc.

The thing is, this time only you have the answer and coaching helps you access that by smashing through the glass ceiling to realize your dreams. Very successful people will tell you about times when they wanted to up-level their skillset or business income and how they had a breakthrough in their mindset before the breakthrough in their business. You see you have to believe its possible and if the wanted outcome is outside your realm of normal thinking or comprehension, then you will need support from someone who can lead you there. That is what the coaching process is all about.

The main reason I wrote this book is to empower people to live their life on purpose. So many of us suffer unnecessarily because we are trying to fit ourselves into someone else's idea of who we should be and make our decisions accordingly. But now we can do it our way, and there doesn't have to be repercussions. The biggest single reason clients come to me is because they aren't living their own life, and they don't understand why they are unhappy. As you know, most of us didn't know what caused us to be this stressed, unhappy, and unfulfilled in the first place—until now. And it is rarely for the reasons we think!

Have you noticed it is much easier to see what someone else is doing wrong than to see what you are doing yourself? Why? Because you have blind spots—sometimes called glass ceilings or filters. You may not be able to see them because of a limiting belief, or because of an emotional attachment that keeps you from seeing. Did you know that you think, hear, speak, and act differently when stressed?

This is why I incorporate the spiritual laws as one of the elements. With the world acting as your mirror and knowing how to read the signs, you can more easily see yourself. Even then it is almost impossible to see clearly always and to know what to do when you do. A lot of us think that we are the way we are, and it can't be changed. You know the saying "A leopard doesn't change its spots." While this is true of the leopard, it doesn't apply to us.

What you are finding out through this book is that there is a good chance the spots you think are yours aren't. This book helps you uncover them. The blame game may have served you for years. Making decisions through your blind spots can be frustrating, as you create the same undesirable results. You may not know what you are doing to make it happen, so you think it is someone else's fault. You may know you are capable of more and ready for more, but you just can't make that step. You may be plagued by uncertainty as to what next.

One of the main reasons individuals come to me for coaching is very simple. They don't know what to do next, and they need help breaking through those limits. Nine out of ten clients come to me because they are stuck. They have run out of ideas for change or have run out of ways to do the same thing and get the same result. What they are most sure of is that they need their current situation to change.

The ability to make clear decisions and to trust in your own decision-making process is golden. Learning to filter through your thoughts/beliefs and emotions to set up your rules will bring a large degree of freedom into your life.

My clients are typically at a pivot point in their life or career where they want to change more than they want to stay the same. Some already excel in their field and are ready to move to the next level—from survival to thriving, even in stressful environments. They have tried to change many times themselves and realize they need help to break through all the different barriers, and glass ceilings they have set up to stay the same. Others excel in their field and struggle with the relationships that are unavoidable as they move up the ladder. The benefits of total intelligence training and developing decision-making skills include the following:

> **You expand your skill set** by developing emotional intelligence and learning to integrate it with your existing skill set.

> **You learn to maintain balance mentally and emotionally in stressful environments,** which is critical to maximizing communication and decision-making skills in those environments.

> **You overcome difficulties in relationships.** Relationships become tricky when you are disconnected or too connected emotionally. The expected behaviors and roles can prevent you from relating to others and instead you relate to who you think the other should be, or what you think he or she should do.

> **You build confidence and self-esteem.** Because you have learned to in-source your acknowledgement, your self-esteem and confidence are no longer based on what others think.

> **You learn to trust yourself and your instincts.** This becomes critical in decision-making and underlies all the other reasons for coaching.

Learning to be the source of your ability to trust yourself and your instincts is invaluable.

➢ **You overcome procrastination and fear.** We are all hardwired for stress leading to a struggle when it comes to planning, scheduling, and prioritizing. When you learn to play your A game under pressure, busy becomes productive.

➢ **You create the space to grow.** It may be that you are ready for that promotion but old patterns have you fighting or fueling fires—instead of showing off your innovative and creative skills to the best of your ability.

➢ **You live life on purpose**—your purpose.

➢ **Change becomes the next natural step** as you learn to navigate using your inner compass.

➢ **You connect with your amazing potential;** swapping the drama for creative projects allows you to tap into talents you never knew you had.

You know and accept your likes and dislikes, and you learn how to express those in a loving way. You begin to choose what you do rather than do it because you should or have to. Your decisions are clear, and when you express them you are listened to because you have learned to speak from total alignment rather than say what you think needs to be said or what you think someone wants to hear. You are empowered with the tools to work your boundaries at all levels, and with practice and time you develop your full potential. The success appears in your outside world, and passion becomes your motivator rather than stress. You shift your way of being from striving to thriving. Your work appears to be easier, giving you more time and space to plan your career and develop relationships to realize your dreams, as you spend less time and energy in fear, knowing how it affects your brain and functioning.

Congratulations!

You are now playing the lead role in your own story! Enjoy!

Resources

On my website, I mention a number of mentors who have made a tremendous difference in my own life and work. While I can't guarantee that they will impact your life in the way they have impacted mine, I certainly recommend you research them for yourself.

To sign up for my free gift and learn more about my programs and how you can work with me, please go to my website
www.thekeanemethod.com

41054297R00112

Made in the USA
Lexington, KY
27 April 2015